David L. Swain, John H. Wheeler, David Fanning, Thomas H. Wynne

The Narrative of Colonel David Fanning

a Tory in the Revolutionary War with Great Britain - giving an account of his adventures in North Carolina, from 1775 to 1783

David L. Swain, John H. Wheeler, David Fanning, Thomas H. Wynne

The Narrative of Colonel David Fanning

a Tory in the Revolutionary War with Great Britain - giving an account of his adventures in North Carolina, from 1775 to 1783

ISBN/EAN: 9783337179861

Printed in Europe, USA, Canada, Australia, Japan

Cover: Foto ©ninafisch / pixelio.de

More available books at **www.hansebooks.com**

"Of such as HE WAS
    There be few on earth :
Of such as HE IS
    There are many in heaven ;
And life is all the sweeter
    That he lived,
And all he loved
    More sacred for his sake ;
And death is all the brighter
    That he died,
And heaven is all the happier
    That he's there."

GEMS OF POETRY AND SONG

ON

JAMES A. GARFIELD.

WITH PORTRAIT AND EULOGY.

God sent his singers upon earth
With songs of sadness and of mirth,
That they might touch the hearts of men
And bring them back to heaven again.
—LONGFELLOW.

COLUMBUS, O.
J. C. McCLENAHAN & COMPANY.
1881.

COPYRIGHTED
By J. C. McClenahan & Co.
1881.

PRESS
COTT & MANN
COLUMBUS

PREFACE.

Whatever is vital to truth and dear to the human heart has found its most attractive expression in poetry. A sublime truth expressed through the medium of the poets is a mighty power for good, "and comes like the benediction that follows after prayer," and is a perpetual spur to noble deeds and illustrious achievements. The thoughts of the great in poetry form part of a nation's intellectual coin, and, like other coin, serve both as the measure and the prolific source of intellectual wealth.

The object of the compiler of the present volume was to collect into a neat form, for preservation, a choice collection of the beautiful sentiments expressed in verse on our beloved and departed President, by the poets of all nations, but more especially those of our own land.

Many of the thoughts herein uttered will remain as lasting memorials "of a fame that never dies," and shall point to the illustrious life of one of God's chosen heroes whose sublimity of character will ever stand as an ideal to all coming

PREFACE.

generations. Heroism and martyrdom have crowned a career unique in modern history.

> "Not on the gory field of fame
>   His noble deeds were done ;
> Not in the sound of earth's acclaim
>   His fadeless crowns were won
> Not from the palaces of kings,
>   Nor fortunes sunny clime,
> Came the great soul, whose life-work flings
>   Lustre o'er earth and time.
>
> "For truth with tireless zeal he sought ;
>   In joyless paths he trod—
> Heedless of praise or blame he wrought,
>   And left the rest to God.
> The lowliest sphere was not disdained ;
>   Where love could soothe or save,
> He went, by fearless faith sustained,
>   Nor knew his deeds were brave."

The amount of poetic literature at hand at this time has enabled us to compile a volume of considerable extent and merit, whereby we bring to the literary market no perishable wares, but the immortal productions of poetic genius in its loftiest aspirations, laying its offerings upon the altars of humanity and pure manhood. The volume is beautifully enriched by a most eloquent and faithful eulogy on the character and work of President Garfield, by Rev. R. S. Storrs, of Brooklyn, New York.

As for our part, we have spared no expense in respect to typography, paper, and mechanical execution, to make the book in appearance equal to its inward merits, and hope that

PREFACE.

we have produced a volume that will justly serve as a memorial to the noble character whose life it seeks to commemorate.

Cordial thanks are due for the courtesy freely extended to us by which several copy-righted poems have been allowed to appear in this collection. In regard to a number of them, permission has been accorded by the authors themselves, and some were written expressly for this work ; other poems have been gathered and have been necessarily used without especial authority, and where due credit is not given, or where the authorship may have been erroneously ascribed, future editions will afford opportunity for correction, which will be gladly made. Particular acknowledgments are offered to the publishers of the following papers and periodicals for the assistance received at their hands: The Boston *Globe*, *Post* and *Transcript*, Cincinnati *Commercial*, Chicago *Tribune* and *Inter-Ocean*, Philadelphia *Times* and *Press*, New York *Tribune*, *Herald*, *Harper's Weekly*, *Harper's Bazaar*, *Leslie's Illustrated Newspaper*, *The Century Magazine*, *Christian at Work*, and *Puck*, London (England) *Spectator*, *Truth*, *Illustrated News*, *Atheneum*, and *Punch*, California *Chronicle*, and many others.

OCTOBER, 1881.   J. C. M.

CONTENTS.

		PAGE
A Burial Ode	T. C. La Moille	99
After The Burial	Oliver Wendell Holmes	27
After All's Done	Miss Muloch	115
After All	Anonymous	31
After The Journey	Anonymous	121
A Hymn	Prof. David Swing	85
A Little While	P. H. Taylor	133
A Letter	John G. Whittier	139
An Exile's Tribute	Mrs. John P. Morgan	98
At The President's Grave	Anonymous	65
At Rest—A Song	B. Herbert	132
Autumn	James A. Garfield	143
Brotherhood	Anonymous	118
Burial of Garfield	Anonymous	130
Carmen Auguratum Auspicans	A. Bronson Alcott	83
Dust to Dust	James Nesbit Karr	114
England to America	London Punch	104
Eulogy	Rev. R. S. Storrs, D. D.	7
Fatherless	Kate Tannatt Woods	93
Garfield	London Punch	82
Garfield—Death Loves a Shining Mark	T. B. Coster	91

CONTENTS.

Garfield's Favorite Hymn................................		138
Garfield President of The People,	*George Parsons Lathrop*	59
Garfield................................	*Anonymous*	61
He is Dead, Our President.......	*Charles Turner Dazey*	72
His First Sabbath in Heaven...............	*S. L. Little*	32
Home at Mentor.............	*Kate Brownlee Sherwood*	34
Illinois to Her Bereaved Sister.................	*Illinois*	55
In Memoriam—The Window—The Grave,	*Rev. J. A. Ely*	36
In Memoriam—James A. Garfield....	*Abbie C. McKeever*	69
In Memoriam.........................	*W. J. Gregg*	22
In Memoriam.........................	*Anonymous*	67
In Memory of General Garfield.............	*Anonymous*	89
In Pace Requiescat.......................	*Anonymous*	44
J. A. G........................	*Julia Ward Howe*	70
J. A. G—Humanitas Regnans............	*M. J. Savage*	77
Laurel—Cypress...............	*Louisa Parsons Hopkins*	24
Lay Him to Sleep.........................	*Anonymous*	101
Lincoln and Garfield..........................	*O. Everts*	81
Memory................................	*James A. Garfield*	141
Midnight......................	*John Boyle O'Reily*	86
Ode to the Assassination...................	*Anonymous*	31
On the Death of President Garfield,	*Paul Hamilton Hayne*	42
One that will be Memorable for Generations,..	*J. W. M.*	45
Our Dead Chief Magistrate...................	*S. A. J.*	111
Our Departed President............	*Alfred Nevin, D. D.*	100
Our Fallen Chief.................	*By an Ex-Confederate*	129
Our Hero................	*Minnie Ward Patterson*	21
President Garfield.........	*Henry Wadsworth Longfellow*	27
President Garfield.......................	*A. C. A.*	49
Queen Victoria's Gift........................	*F. D.*	48

Queen Victoria's Wreath	George W. Ferrel	63
Rejoice	Joaquin Miller	50
Requiem	Mrs. Laura G. W. White	52
September 19, 1881	Thomas Bailey Aldrich	66
Sleep, Comrade!	Anonymous	126
Sonnet—James A. Garfield	H. Bernard Carpenter	113
Strange Craft in the Offing	Lilly C. Darst	137
The Calling of the Roll on High	Anonymous	125
The Dead President	S. H. Thayer	117
The End	John G. Holland	26
The Fire is Out	F. W. C.	23
The Greed for Office	Edward Berwick	102
The Last Bulletin	Maria E. Blake	95
The Lord Reigneth	E. F. L. Gauss	124
The Nation Weeps	Joseph A. Nunez	105
The Nation's Guide	George Bird-Eye	108
The Night of Death	Rudolph Elstein Ugiets	82
The Second Martyr	D. M. Jones	74
The Sobbing of the Bells	Walt Whitman	113
The Soldier by the Sea	David Graham Adee	60
The Sorrow of the Nations	Thomas MacKellar	107
There is Mourning Everywhere	Anonymous	109
They Loved Him	Eugene J. Hall	122
Thou Knowest Best	F. W. Reeder	135
Time's Hand Shall Comfort Us	Lucy M. Creemer	134
To Mrs. Garfield	Theodore Watts	85
Why Should They Kill My Baby	Will Carleton	119
Why Should We Mourn	Anonymous	81
Young Garfield at Chattanooga	Hezekiah Butterworth	96

EULOGY ON JAMES ABRAM GARFIELD.

By Rev. R. S. Storrs, D. D.

He who has died by the stroke of the assassin, or by the unjust stroke of power, having filled high offices and honorably filled them, has always commanded thereby the reverence of mankind. William of Orange and Henry Fourth of France, illustrate this to us; our own Lincoln, as clearly as any in all the past. The statues of Counts Egmont and Horn stand in the great square at Brussels in which they were executed, before the windows through which Alva looked unrelentingly on their death. The blood of Walter Raleigh, killed by the jealous and tyrannical James, makes enduring imprint upon history, and only allures men to closer study of his chivalrous career. And so shall it be in coming time with him for whose untimely death, at the hand of a mean and malicious assassin, the world mourns. That on the brightest, gladdest day of all his life, at the summit of his power and hope, the bullet smote him, will keep his name eminent before the eyes of mankind.

But even aside altogether from this tragic pathos of its end, there has been that in the life of our late President which will be sure to give him a prominent place in history. It is certainly unequalled in the rapidity of the changes which make it read almost like a romance, like some ancient poetic fancy solidified in the modern American experience. Think of the marvellous and swift changes in that career, now so suddenly and so sadly closed! Born in a log house in 1831, in the then remote State of Ohio, in a comparatively unsettled district of that State; losing his father at the age of eighteen months, so that he could never afterwards remember his father's face; accustomed to see his mother working in the fields as well as in the house, and to hear her read her four chapters in the Bible every day; at the age of fourteen helping to build the first frame house for that mother, replacing the previous one of logs with one more comfortable; at the age of sixteen driving horses on the tow-path on the canal; at the age of eighteen, under the strong impression of religious truth and the strong impulse of the faith in his heart, uniting himself to the Church, under whose history and teaching he had been brought up; still later, going to school to fit himself for college if that might be; living for a time on thirty-one cents a week, which was all that he had for food; working as a carpenter, that he might pay his tuition, and buy for himself some necessary books; finally received into college, and spending his two years there with profit and in honor, having entered in advance of the class; in 1856 entering political discussion and public activity for the first time, of course in a modest and humble way, in what is known as the Fremont campaign; returning to marry two years later the woman to whom his heart had been pledged, whose studies he had by turns guided and shared, and in whom his heart most safely trusted—in whom the heart of this nation has now delight, and shall have evermore; unable by reason of his poverty to secure or build a house for himself and family until four years later; becoming principal in instruction in the school from which he had gone to college; becoming a member of one branch of the State Legislature; entering the army in 1861; Lieutenant-Colonel; then Colonel; then Brigadier-General; then Major-General, until in the close of 1863 he resigned his place in the army in order to enter Congress, to which he had been elected without solicitation or previous expectation on his part, and which he was earnestly urged by Mr. Lincoln, then President, to enter, that his military experience, as well as his civil wisdom and eloquence, might be of service to the government in Congress; re-elected nine times, and associated with the different important committees, on Ways and Means, on Military Affairs, on Banking and Currency, and on Appropriations; the leader of his party in the House, unchallenged at last in that position; elected to the Senate; before he had time to be seated as Senator elected President—and all before he had reached the age of fifty years! Bring into one view that crowded, changing career, so full of resolute endurance and fortitude, of courage and persistent endeavor, so full of success—rapid, signal, victorious success—until, beginning so humbly and closing on such heights of power and renown, this amazing career was to be crowned—has been crowned—and baptized into sacredness by the blow of the assassin! I think we shall all concede it as certain that history will keep the remembrance of his name! Even as the fame of Washington has not been obscured or lowered, as the generations have passed; as the fame of Lincoln seems sure to be the same while the country endures; so the fame of this man, just gone from us, will only be brighter and higher as years go on.

And there are some things which I am sure that the general sense of the country and of the world will affirm concerning this man, as his character and work, and the story of his life, are longer and more carefully pondered. Certainly the history which keeps the record of his career will recognize the fact that he was the most conspicuous representative, in his generation, of a complete and genuine American manhood. In his blood he represented the commingled and powerful life of the people. His ancestors were English, with a sprinkling possibly, of Welsh blood in their veins. An early intermarriage united them with the German stock For more than two centuries and a third, I believe, they had been in this country. One of them had been in the Concord fight, where was fired the shot "heard around the world." After the Revolution they removed to the interior of this great State. At the beginning of this century, under the impulse which pushes always Americans westward, they removed again to Ohio; and there, through his mother, came to the boy who was afterwards to be President, an infusion of that Huguenot blood which has added so much of the splendid and the noble to our public history; the blood represented by Jay, and Boudinot, and Bowdoin, and the Bayards, by Laurens and Huger, and all the others. I think this gave to the boy in Ohio his sensibility, his tastefulness, something of special courage and aspiration, with not a little of his surpassing fervid eloquence.

He represented thus, in the very genesis of his life, the elements which go to form the strenuous American life-force. He represented as well, in both his early and later training, the discipline which has trained that essential life-force into beauty and power. All the small means of general culture which were accessible to General Garfield in youth were just those common to American children: the district school, the modest academy, a few newspapers and books. In the use of these began the knowledges, by aid of these were developed the powers which afterwards were displayed in his manhood. Therefore it was, in part, at least, that his sympathy was so wide with all classes of men. Whether of one nationality or race, or of another, whether of one condition in life or another, there were none who were not received by him with most ready and cordial welcome. By birth and training he was brother to all.

He represented the American in his readiness for every department of work. In civil life, or in military life, he was ready for the demands of any office when those demands were made upon him. He had not been born of an aristocratic stock, the influences of which had predetermined him to one career only. If he had been incapacitated from any cause, while in office, for other pursuits, he could have earned his living on the farm—he enjoyed his farming life better than he did his public career. As a preacher, as a legislator in the halls of Congress, as General in the army, or as President, his aim was always to do the best that he could do, with all his force, while in the station, and to be ready to go from it to any other when time was ripe. That fitness and instant readiness to meet the demands of any office entrusted to him insured a far wider range of influence than he otherwise could have reached.

In his natural and strong tendency toward public life, his desire to imprint his impressions, if he might, on the affairs of the country, he represented the spirit which is common in our Republican nation. We sometimes criticise it; we ask why it is that any man with the wealth of moral and mental resource which this man had, wants to enter public office. It is because he sees the large relations of the influence which he there may exert. In this democratic country the desire for public office is to the best man a just, laudable, and beneficent ambition. He represented the American spirit in that very thing; and in the passion of patriotism, which is not with the intelligent American the mere love of a particular territory, because he happened to be born upon that territory, which is the immense and religious enthusiasm born of the past history of the nation, of its grand works, its grand endurances, and of the vast and bright opportunities opening before it. Therefore the nation honors him now with this universal grief and praise. Therefore it stands with its tearful eyes looking after him as he ascends into the heavens; and feels that "we have lost our bravest, our fairest, and our best," in whom was incarnated the vital genius of the expanding American people at the present time.

I do not think that Washington, if he were alive to-day, and in his old office, would be accepted as such a representative of the public spirit as now it exists. He stands apart, reserved, and comparatively exceptional; representing the magnificent class of Virginia planters of his time—a class whose work and power were indispensable to the success of the popular cause in the war of Revolution, but which was essentially a special class in American society. He does not represent, as this man who so sadly passed from us has done, the popular temper of even his own time. Lincoln did not represent it in all his relations, although in some more vividly even than he who has gone. But Lincoln did not touch the rarer and finer culture of his time. He had been educated with Shakespeare, and Burns, and the Bible, but he was not a linguist like Garfield, who had accomplished his desire to make himself master of the different languages toward which his spirit had early been drawn. With the classical languages, with the modern literary languages of the world, he had made himself familiar. In the compass of his mind and attainment he touched the extremes of American life; and while at home in thought as well as feeling, with the ploughman in the field or the mechanic in the shop, he was equally at home with the Professor in his class-room, and with the deep and subtle thinker in his finest analysis of thought or life.

So he stands before us in the fullness of that character and generous culture which our times, in our country, cherish and demand; and I think that, if only in this respect, as representing so vividly the genuine and complete American manhood, we might well mourn his loss more than for all the eloquence which we know to have been so often on his lips, more than for all the wisdom in counsel which was expected from him in the future conduct of the government. I think, too, that it cannot be doubted that the story of his astonishing career will contribute to further this manhood throughout the nation. What he became, and what he did throughout his life, will be brighter now, since he is dead, since the red crown of martyrdom fell upon him. He has done as much, at least, as any man of his time, to advance and foster true manhood in his country. He aimed to do this, as far as he had opportunity, with a particular and positive purpose. In his work as a preacher, his object was to touch and ennoble the moral nature of man. He studied to do it as an educator. One who was under him has testified to that affectionate fidelity with which the honored instructor followed him after his school hours, mingling with his pupils familiarly, and, at the same time, asserting his dignity in the school room in a manner impressive to all. As a soldier, he was humane and generous, as well as chivalrous and daring. He was working for moral ends, even amid the fierce and stubborn clash of arms; not only for the maintenance of the old national institutions, but for the furtherance of the noble moral life of the nation, which seemed to him essential to the maintenance of those institutions and the re-establishment of national unity. He fought, not from desire for military aggrandizement, but impelled to the fight, as so many other unnumbered thousands were, by the inward moral impulse which affirmed the unbroken American Union necessary to the sustenance of the highest moral and Christian life throughout the country.

In legislation, his aim uniformly was to maintain justice, equity, and honesty, in order that the moral life of the nation might be educated by its law-making and law-makers. We may not always apprehend—I doubt if we do—how much the character of a people is moulded by the laws which it in its freedom allows or enacts. It educates and inspires, as well as expresses, its highest reason and conscience in just laws. Precisely in proportion as such laws affirm the dominance of principles of righteousness above present convenience, interest, or pleasure, they are salutary to the heart and moral sense of a nation. More than essays, poems, art, they cultivate and strengthen whatever is best in it; and our late President—when a legislator he insisted on paying honest debts in honest money, not in currency, but in gold—was educating the spirit and heart-life of the people; and when he advocated with equal earnestness and power, or carried out to equal accomplishment, other measures of difficult public equity and virtue, the nation in its ruling majority had taken a fresh oath, by reason of his impression upon it, to fidelity and righteousness, to the future, and to God.

But more than as an educator, soldier, preacher, or legislator, he has educated, and will educate in time to come, the moral life of the people by the character he exhibited. I do not doubt that he had his frailties and faults, though what they were I am not aware; but we cannot be mistaken in feeling that the combination in him of gentleness and of courage, of the most resolute fortitude and the most uncomplaining patience, of the sweetest domestic affection and the highest patriotic consecration, all crowned with religious devotion and faith—this combination has been remarkable—I will not say unique, but very signal. Among all the public men whose names we reckon upon the rolls of our illustrious when we read our history, there has been no one who has stood nearer the Christian judgment and heart of the land. There has been no one, therefore, from whom an influence has emanated, finer in its nature, or wider in its reach. He who incarnates character exerts more power for good than he who teaches about it. It is a glory to our history that such a character has appeared, with such a training and in such a position, to be celebrated here in time to come. The great leaders of the State have always this illustrious office, of training to like quality with themselves the men, especially the young men, who admire and follow their brilliant lead. We know how much Jackson did in this way, with his masterful will; how much Webster, with his magnificent eloquence; or Clay, with his daring and chivalrous leadership. We know how much Washington has done thus from the outset, with his unyielding supremacy of spirit. So the influence of this man is to pass into the future. He has passed where our praises or tears can no more move him, but this homage of the land has had in it a solace and succor for him in all his fierce protracted trial; and it has come to the character which he has exhibited most clearly in these last sad and memorable and most instructive weeks. I think it better for the country to have had that character exhibited in its ruler than to have had him most signally successful in any measures of public policy; better and nobler for him to have shown it than if he had voiced his thought in any chiming poetic stanzas, than if he had elaborated any treatise, or builded with artistic grace the grandest cathedral. It is an immense and consummating work, to have interfused the impulses of his character and career, by the universal homage which has crowned them, into the unfolding life of the American people.

Especially, let us not forget how he has led the civilized world, through the peculiar circumstances of his career, to know and to honor American domestic life and personal character as it never had done before. The power of the American people had been before and increasingly recognized throughout the realms of the civilized world. Our vast civil war was at least a challenge to the attention of mankind, showing what military power was here, and what ample resources of money and skill, and of will to use them. The vast and rapid increase of wealth, the astonishing multiplication of the products of invention, the steady progress of the nation for a hundred years in order and in liberty—all these had impressed the peoples, and even the princes of the earth, with a sense of the growing American power. But what has been best and most characteristic in private and social life here has had less chance of any general recognition. The outside world never could understand the sweetness, purity, and domestic felicity of the American family. Now for the first time Europe understands what American social life really is. Here is a plain, Christian household, suddenly and most unexpectedly lifted from private life to the highest position, made the focus on which are turned the converging thoughts and regards of the world; and through the long period of suffering of him who is its head, from the bullet of the assassin, every word and action in that household has been audible and evident to the circles of mankind; and there has not been one to be criticised or lamented. Living in the blaze of such publicity as almost no other household has known, mother and children have been those that we would fain have chosen to represent our families to the world! Here is a man whose name had been unheard in England, and in other countries, until he was nominated for the office which he so honorably filled. Tender in his affection, wise in his counsel, modest and yet courageous and confident concerning his position, from the first of his sickness to the last of it there is not a word uttered by him, there is not an expression of feeling or thought, that we would have changed if we had had the opportunity. This was almost the grandest office that any man ever has had to accomplish for this country.

History will say then, as long as she preserves his name, that he represented fully and vividly the American spirit; that he encouraged that spirit, by his example as well as his work; that he interpreted American life to the world at large, and brought the world to recognize and honor it. Therefore he is recognized as a kind of mediator between the Christian people on this side of the Atlantic and the Christian people on the other; who has interpreted to them what is deepest in our spiritual life, who has inspired their sympathy toward us—touching the sensitive heart of the world, which mines of silver do not touch, which great battles do not touch, which great debates do not touch, but which suffering, bravely and patiently borne, character magnanimously and magnificently revealed—alone could have reached. He has positively bound the civilized peoples in new bonds of kindliness and of friendship.

One other thing of still grander significance has been accomplished by the President in his dying, for the people to whose welfare his life was devoted. He has brought it nearer, in faith and prayer, to the God whom he worshipped, and has taught it where alone its true strength may be found! No bullet smites the life of God. No change or waste diminishes His eternal vigor. On Him alone can peoples rest. Hang the planet on the sun and it swings in serene tranquility in its orbit. Try to suspend it on any palace or forum or church which man has builded, and how surely would it rush into nether abysses? Hang the hope of the nation on God, who has shown such marvellous providence toward us in the past, and we are at rest; suspend it on the life and power of any man, the grandest, noblest of the land, and we have no hope that can be really secure and inspiring.

With this new sense of the dependence of the nations upon God, and of the common spiritual life which thrills sympathetically on such an occasion around the world, whatsoever is fraternal and affectionate in our spirit, public or personal, should take a new impulse. Let us clasp hands around the grave of him who has passed from our supreme place; who has joined the North and South, laying his dying hands upon them both, and saying: " Be friends forevermore!" and let us hear his voice from the heavens: " All you who are united in love and homage toward me, a mortal ascended to the heavens, be united in love, fraternal in affection and sympathy toward each other! Let your union be consecrated by my death and ascension! And forevermore dwell in joyful and intimate mutual esteem, and in common patriotic service and hope!"

And as toward all in our own land, so toward the countries across the sea. We have hated England; we have writhed beneath her taunts sometimes; we have scorned her patronizing sympathy. But now, when from the Queen on the throne to the humblest assembly of mechanics, come messages of tender sympathy with our beloved Presidential family, with all the American people stricken by the loss of their chief magistrate, how we recognize the true unity of the nation on that side and this!

As a closing word, let us remember as we travel onward what was the most precious of all things to him who is departed! He held great offices, accomplished great successes; in life he was crowned with all the honors which the land of his birth has to bestow. When strength was failing, and life was ending, he must have felt that the great heart of the nation, swelling and praying around his bedside, was the reward for every endeavor he ever had made and every sacrifice he had ever endured. But above all that, above the love of friends, above the love of the wife of his heart, was the anticipation of immortality through the love and grace of God. In one of the illustrated papers is a picture, singularly touching and beautiful, which represents him sitting by the window at Elberon, and gazing out upon the sea. He looked across it to another sea, of vaster expanse, of clearer glory! By gentlest hands, with carefulest skill, he who there sat had been brought without pain or jar thus far on his way to the Home beyond. By trains more noiseless and more swift, under the ministry of tenderer gentleness and of more celestial and consummate skill, God took him up to his immortal abiding-place. We sorrow for ourselves, but not for him! The faith in Christ which was with him the central fact of spirit and life, has now become vision, peace, and Paradise! He stands henceforth, redeemed and purified, through Him who loved him, in tranquil felicity, with illustrious companions, "the glory and honor of the nations," among the immortal Sons of Light!

GEMS OF POETRY AND SONG.

OUR HERO.

Alas! for Columbia, her chieftain low lying
   No more wields the scepter her tower and her pride,
No solace but this for our heart's heavy sighing—
   A hero he lived and a hero he died!

At first, through the dark, mazy jungle of learning,
   He crept or he leaped to the sunlight of truth,
All barriers dispelling, discouagement spurning—
   The Garfield we mourn was a hero in youth!

When Wrong and Oppression held sway in our borders,
   And the wild southern war-cloud ensanguined the sky,
Obedient he sprang to his dear country's orders,
   His strong heart determined to conquer or die!

At the semblance of peace, in the hush of war-clamor,
   His genius and courage his countrymen claimed;
His keen eye detected the perilous glamour—
   To dispel it, heroic the efforts he aimed;

On field and on forum, in peace and in riot,
  His learning, discretion and valor rose high;
But grander the hero in Elberon quiet
  Who showed how a patriot and Christian can die!

So thin is the veil at the portal Elysian,
  So pure was the man, with the angels who trod,
Transfigured he lived in the light of a vision,
  And felt the heart throbs of the Infinite God!

Oh! bright be the bloom by the summer wind shaken,
  And green be the sod where his ashes repose;
For the name of our hero forever shall waken
  The homage of friends and the honor of foes!

This grave be the Mecca through myriad ages,
  Where pilgrims shall gather with reverent feet!
This life be a star upon history's pages,
  Where the glory of power and of gentleness meet!
                                  Minnie Ward Patterson.

IN MEMORIAM.

Bow down, my soul! a nation mourns her chief,
  A stricken people bend beneath the rod;
Auspicious hope gives place to hopeless grief,
  And strong hearts faint beneath the heavy load.

Farewell, great heart! a long and last farewell!
  A world, still hoping, watched thy latest breath:
A world in sorrow hears thy funeral knell;
  A world in anguish yields thee up to death.

Thou art not dead! God's chosen cannot die,
  Thy loving words yet fill our waiting ears;
Thy noble deeds on memory's page shall lie,
  Undimmed and fadeless by the flight of years.

Blest be thy name! thy memory ever blest;
  A nation bends in homage at thy tomb.
Thy godly life, a nation's rich bequest;
  Thy Christian death a flower of fadeless bloom.

O God! to Thee, Controller of events,
  We bring our land in this her bitter hour;
Be Thou her Rock, her refuge and defense;
  Guide Thou the Ship of State by Thy great power.
                              W. J. Gregg.

THE FIRE IS OUT.

September 19, 1881.

The bell struck once. "The fire is out,"
  The listening people said.
Again the stroke, and yet again!
  The President was dead!

Throughout the night the clanging bells
  Retold their tale of woe.
"The fire is out!" Ah! long that flame
  Had flickered dim and low.

"The fire is out!" So rang the bells;
  Our hearts grew sick and cold;
A sleeping city waked to hear
  The message that they told.

Out! from the weary, wasted frame;
  Out! from that kindly eye.
Oh, bravely must the man have lived
  Who could so bravely die.

"The fire is out!" But the dust remains;
  Yet over it shall rise
The tribute of a Nation's love;
  The fame that never dies.

                               F. W. C.

LAUREL—CYPRESS.

March 4, 1881.

He stands at the Capitol's portal
  With lifted hand.
The vows of God are upon him
  For the trust of the land;
  Chief true and grand!

His manhood turns in its glory
    To womanhood.
To his wife and mother he yearns
    From the multitude;
    Heart true and good!

He crowns them before the people
    With kiss of love.
See it, ye men, and shout,
      Full hearts will out;
      Rend the heavens above!

September 23, 1881.

He lies in the wide rotunda
    With folded palms;
"Wounded for our transgressions."
    Comrades in arms,
    Spread ye his pall,
    For the peace of all!

The thronging crowds have passed him,
    With falling tear;
A queenly woman's garland
    Upon his bier;
    Knight without fear,
    Man brave and dear!

In this his martyr-glory
    Leave him alone ;
For his kiss-crowned wife is coming,
    Though dead—he has known
    She would come—his own—
    To share his throne.
            Louisa Parsons Hopkins.

THE END.

A wasp flew out upon our fairest son
    And stung him to the quick with poisoned shaft ;
    The while he chatted carelessly and laughed,
And knew not of the fatal mischief done.
And so this life, amid our love begun,
    Envenomed by the insect's hellish craft,
    Was drunk by death in one long, feverish draught,
And he was lost—the precious, priceless one !
    Oh, mystery, of blind, remorseless fate !
    Oh, cruel end of a most causeless hate !
    That life so mean should murder life so great !
What is there left to us who think and feel,
Who have no remedy and no appeal,
But damn the wasp and crush him under heel ?
            J. G. Holland.

PRESIDENT GARFIELD.

"E VENNI DAL MARTARIO A QUESTA PACE."

These words the poet heard in Paradise,
  Uttered by one who, bravely dying here,
  In the true faith was living in that sphere
Where the Celestial Cross of sacrifice
Spread its protecting arms athwart the skies;
  And, set thereon like jewels crystal clear,
  The souls magnanimous, that knew not fear,
Flashed their effulgence on his dazzled eyes.

Ah, me! how dark the discipline of pain,
  Were not the suffering followed by the sense
  Of infinite rest and infinite release!
This is our consolation; and again
  A great soul cries to us in our suspense:
  "I came from martyrdom unto this peace!"
Henry W. Longfellow.

AFTER THE BURIAL.

I.

Fallen with autumn's falling leaf
  Ere yet his summer's noon was past,
Our friend, our guide, our trusted chief—
  What words can match a woe so vast!

And whose the chartered claim to speak
 The sacred grief where all have part,
When sorrow saddens every cheek
 And broods in every aching heart?

Yet Nature prompts the burning phrase
 That thrills the hushed and shrouded hall,
The loud lament, the sorrowing praise,
 The silent tear that love lets fall.

In loftiest verse, in lowliest rhyme
 Shall strive unblamed the minstrel choir,—
The singers of the newborn time
 And trembling age with outworn lyre.

No room for pride, no place for blame—
 We fling our blossoms on the grave,
Pale,—scentless,—faded,—all we claim,
 This only—what we had we gave.

Ah, could the grief of all who mourn
 Blend in one voice its bitter cry,
The wail to heaven's high arches borne
 Would echo through the caverned sky.

II.

O happiest land whose peaceful choice
 Fills with a breath its empty throne!
God, speaking through thy people's voice,
 Has made that voice for once his own.

No angry passion shakes the State
   Whose weary servant seeks for rest,—
And who could fear that scowling hate
   Would strike at that unguarded breast?

He stands, unconscious of his doom,
   In manly strength, erect, serene—
Around him summer spreads her bloom;
   He falls—what horror clothes the scene!

How swift the sudden flash of woe
   Where all was bright as childhood's dream!
As if from heaven's etherial bow
   Had leaped the lightning's arrowy gleam.

Blot the foul deed from history's page,
   Let not the all-betraying sun
Blush for the day that stains an age
   When murder's blackest wreath was won.

III.

Pale on his couch the sufferer lies,
   The weary battle-ground of pain;
Love tends his pillow, science tries
   Her every art, alas! in vain.

The strife endures how long! how long!
   Life, death, seemed balanced in the scale,
While round his bed a viewless throng
   Awaits each morrow's changing tale.

In realms the desert ocean parts
   What myriads watch with tear-filled eyes,
His pulsebeats echoing in their hearts,
   His breathings counted with their sighs!

Slowly the stores of life are spent,
   Yet hope still battles with despair,
Will heaven not yield when knees are bent?
   Answer, O Thou that hearest prayer!

But silent is the brazen sky, —
   On sweeps the meteor's threatening train, —
Unswerving Nature's mute reply,
   Bound in her adamantine chain.

Not ours the verdict to decide
   Whom death shall claim or skill shall save;
The hero's life though Heaven denied
   It gave our land a martyr's grave.

Nor count the teaching vainly sent
   How human hearts their griefs may share, —
The lesson woman's love has lent
   What hope may do, what faith can bear!

Farewell! the leaf strown earth enfolds
   Our stay, our pride, our hopes, our fears,
And autumn's golden sun beholds
   A nation bowed, a world in tears.

Oliver Wendell Holmes.

AFTER ALL.

Despite the prayers and tears, and earnest pleading,
    And piteous protest o'er a hero's fall,
Despite the hopeful signs, our hearts misleading,
    Death cometh after all!

Over the brightest scenes are clouds descending;
    The flame soars highest ere its deepest fall;
The glorious day has all too swift an ending;
    Night cometh after all!

O'er bloom or beauty now in our possession
    Is seen the shadow of the funeral pall;
Though Love and Life make tearful intercession,
    Death cometh after all!

---

*ODE TO THE ASSASSINATION.

Veil, now, O Liberty, thy blushing face,
    At the fell deed that thrills a startled world;
When fair Columbia weeps in dire disgrace
    And bows in sorrow o'er the banner furled.

---

* A prize offered by a London weekly for the best poem on the assassination of President Garfield, was awarded to the author of these verses.

No graceless tyrant falls by Vengeance here,
  'Neath the wild justice of the secret knife;
Nor red Ambition ends its grim career,
  And expiates its horrors with its life.

Not here does rash Revenge, misguided, burn
  To free a nation from the assassin's dart:
Or roused Despair in angry madness turn,
  And tear its freedom from the despot's heart.

But where blest Liberty so widely reigns,
  And Peace and Plenty make a smiling land:
Here the mad wretch its fair, white record stains,
  And blurs its beauty with a bloody hand.

Here the elect of millions, and the pride
  Of those who own his mild and peaceful rule—
Here Virtue sinks and yields the crimson tide,
  Beneath the vile unreason of a fool.

HIS FIRST SABBATH IN HEAVEN.

How calm is the glow of this first Sabbath morn,
  Since with hearts stricken down in their grief,
In his palm-covered coffin we laid him away—
  Our martyred illustrious chief.

What a change since his last suffering Sabbath on earth—
  Those groans for that rapturous song
Which only the ransomed of Jesus can know—
  The blood washed! the glorified throng!

The victor in Christ over death has prevailed!
  And oh, how divine his reward!
Without one faint shadow he seeth unvailed
  The glorious face of the Lord.

Oh, vision of visions! the sight of that face
  Would for ages of misery atone!
The lovely Redeemer of Adam's lost race—
  The conqueror of Death on His throne!

Were the gates left ajar as he passed to his rest?
  Were some wandering rays downward borne?
Such a heavenly radiance seems to invest
  The skies on his first Sabbath morn.

But, chastened and sorrowing nation, oh learn
  The lessons our Father would give;
From the ways that have grieved his good spirit return,
  Repent, seek His mercy and live.

Then for the bright light now removed from our skies,
  That has left us in darkness to mourn,
New stars for our hope and our guidance shall rise,
  Till breaks the millennial dawn.

S. L. Little.

HOME AT MENTOR.

"O this is wondrous sweet!
To rest so stilly in the long green grass,
And watch the lake blown vapors as they pass;
  To catch the throb and beat
   Of busy baby feet,
And feel myself once more at home, at home,
No more beside the fateful sea to roam,
    Sweet Mentor home!

  "I have had bitter strife—
Some hateful dream. Me seemed some evil thing
Came swift behind as I was hastening
  To clasp my poor, pale wife,
   Wrestling so sore for life,
And stung me like an adder, so I lay
And longed for home and Mentor day by day,
    Sweet Mentor home!

  "Me seemed this slimy thing
Wound round and round me with its loathsome touch,
So that I sighed, and sobbed, and sorrowed much,
  That none would come to wrest
   Its fangs from off my breast,
And I set my feet once more toward the spot
That I have cherished in my holiest thought,
    Sweet Mentor home!

"And as the day went by
The awful horror slowly crept and crept ;
My stricken heart stood still, or wildly leapt ;
    My flesh grew parched and dry ;
    There rose a dimness even to my eye,
That like the eagle's had withstood the sun,
My feeble lips scarce name a name save one,
    Sweet Mentor home!

"O blessed home! Come reach
That book, my Mollie, that you love so well—
The Charles and Mary Lamb—let Shakespeare tell
    His matchless stories through their gentler speech ;
    And as I read, my boys, sit silent each,
While Grandmama beside me smiles and knits,
And busy with her cares our mother flits—
    Sweet Mentor home!

"O this is rest, I ween !
After the storm and strife the cloudless calm,
After the stifling streets, the breath of balm ;
    The slopes of living green,
    The daisied dells atween ;
The bending, blessing Buckeye sky above
Around, the sheltering arms of sylvan love ;
    Sweet Mentor home !"

    O happy, happy soul !
What Hope came down to kiss thy dying eyes,

And bid thy dear old home before thee rise?
    What whispering voice
    Bids us rejoice,
That after life's sad dreaming has been past,
There comes the vision of our rest at last?
    Sweet Mentor home!
        Kate Brownlee Sherwood.

IN MEMORIAM.

AT THE WINDOW.

Elberon, N. J., Sept. 13 and Sept. 20, 1881.
Beside the window, looking o'er the sea,
He lay, on whom the people's heart was set
    As never yet
The hearts of millions in the mystery
Of love and longing to one heart were bound;
    Encompassing him 'round
With ceaseless vigil, till each whispered word
    The wide world heard
And every weary groan
Was echoed by a nation's sympathising moan.

Beside the window looking o'er the sea
He lay, in that unequal fight with death;
    And every breath
That blew across his couch we prayed might be

A minister of strength to him again
           And victory over pain,
As in his heart he felt anew the joy
           That as a boy
Was his, when on his dreams
The far-off ocean rose to tempt him with its gleams.

Beside the window looking o'er the sea
He lay, and heard the restless billows roar
           Along the shore ;
And far across the waves where silently
The distant waters stretched, his eager eye
           Sought the encircling sky,
Or lingered where with snowy wings outspread
           The swift ships sped
Nor knew whose longing gaze
Was following them, unseen, upon their devious ways.

Beside the window looking o'er the sea
He lay, but uttered not what thoughts awoke,
           What voices spoke,
Through those days shadowed by eternity,
Within his struggling heart. Yet as a star
           In silence from afar
Sheds o'er the heaving deep that lies below
           Its tranquil glow,
So on his troubled breast
The light of some far realm of quiet seemed to rest.

Beside the window looking o'er the sea
He lay, nor knew that all the world was bright
      With that soft light
Of love and courage, strength and purity,
That from his chamber with such radiance streams
      To cast its cheering beams
O'er every sufferer's path and show the way
      Through night to day,
And 'mid the wrecks of earth
Disclose the budding honors of immortal birth.

Beside the window looking o'er the sea
He lay, and felt anew each earthly bond
      And every fond
Affection of his home more tenderly
Because so soon to part. And all his hope
      Grew wider in its scope
At that fell touch which turned it all to dust,
      And yet in trust
He yielded to his doom
And with unfaltering step went downward to the tomb.

Beside the window looking o'er the sea
He lay, eyes closed and hand upon the breast
      At last at rest.
Without the changeless ocean ceaselessly

Sobbed on the beach, but not for him its wail ;
        His honors cannot fail ;
The stars of earthly fame that burn for him
        Can ne'er grow dim :
For us the mournful cry
Who seek in vain below that which has passed on high.

Beside the window looking o'er the sea
He lies no more ; to-day with loving hand
        Far from the strand,
  Amid a nation's grief his form will be
Laid in its grave ; but his heroic soul
        So fashioned to control,
Enthroned above among the eternal spheres,
        Through distant years,
Ruling with gentle sway,
Shall guide the land he loved upon its onward way.

Beside the window looking o'er the sea
He still shall lie, wearing his sorrow's crown ;
        And gazing down,
As from pure realms of light, with vision free,
Across the troubled waves of human life
        And all its bitter strife,
The noise of faction at his feet shall cease,
        Awed into peace ;
And purified by pain
The stricken nation from his death new life shall gain.

AT THE GRAVE.

Cleveland, O., September 26, 1881.

The spring of hope has changed for us
    To autumn's dull decay,
The summer bloom and sweet perfume
    Seem now so far away.

Was ever earth so bright and fair?
    Was ever hope so high?
Did angel song once float along
    A clear and tranquil sky?

Did time seem turning back once more
    To bring the age of gold,
When peace on earth, of heavenly birth
    Good will to men foretold?

So dark to-day the heavens are hung,
    The world so changed and sad,
That like a dream those visions seem
    Of days that once were glad.

With weary step and troubled heart
    We wander to and fro,
While all the strife of human life
    Seems like an idle show.

Was it for this, our spirits cry,
    He felt the sacred fire,
And caught new light from every height,
    To draw the world's desire?

Was it for this, from low degree
    He wrought through toilsome years,
And won the crown of great renown,
    And sat among his peers?

Was it for this that wisdom came,
    And skill and gentle force,
That brave and good at last he stood
    To guide the nation's course?

The seas lay calm about the prow,
    No storm-cloud hung behind,
He gave the word, the vessel heard
    And leaped before the wind.

Ah! who could deem that danger lurked
    Within those peaceful skies;
With sudden shock the heart of rock
    Is rent, and prostrate lies!

A thousand swords had left their sheath
    That life from ill to guard,
From countless fields unnumbered shields
    Had leaped to be his ward.

Had there been one, but only one
    Of all that mighty host,
Our leader slain, were ours again
    And ruling at his post.

It could not be ; a nation's tears
  Must mourn a nation's guilt;
And factious strife must plunge the knife
  Of murder to the hilt.

God pity and forgive us all
  For bitter thought and speech;
God in His love look from above
  And heal his people's breach.

Then, from the tears we shed to-day
  About his open tomb,
In summer hours perennial flowers
  Shall spring in deathless bloom.

Sweet flowers of peace o'er all the land
  Shall God in mercy sow,
To wreathe the brow, so anguished now,
  That for our sakes lays low.

Rev. Jospeh A. Ely.

ON THE DEATH OF PRESIDENT GARFIELD.

I see the Nation, as in antique ages,
  Crouched with rent robes, and ashes on her head;
Her mournful eyes are deep with dark presages,
  Her soul is haunted by a formless dread!

"O God!" she cries, "why hast Thou left me bleeding,
   Wounded and quivering to the heart's hot core?
Can fervid faith, winged prayer, and anguished pleading
   Win balm and pity from Thy heavens no more?

"I knelt, I yearned, in agonizing passion,
   Breathless to catch Thy 'still small voice' from far;
Now Thou *hast* answered, but in awful fashion,
   And stripped our midnight of its last pale star.

"What tears are given me in o'ermastering measure,
   From fathomless floods of Marah, darkly free,
While that pure life I held my noblest treasure
   Is plunged forever in death's tideless sea!

"Hark to those hollow sounds of lamentation,
   The muffled music, the funereal bell;
From far and wide on wings of desolation
   Float wild and wailful voices of farewell.

"The North-land mourns her grief in full libation,
   Outpoured for him who died at Victory's goal;
And the great West, in solemn ministration,
   May not recall her hero's shining soul.

"Yea, the North mourns; the West, a stricken mother,
   Droops as in sackcloth with veiled brow and mouth;
And what old strifes, what waning hates, can smother
   The generous heart-throbs of the pitying South?

"Did doubt remain?—*she* crushed its latest ember
   At that stern moment when the victim's fall
Changed loveliest summer to a grim December,
   Paled by the hiss of Guiteau's murderous ball.

"Thus by the spell of one vast grief united
   (Where cypress boughs their death-cold shadows wave).
My sons, I trust, a holier faith have plighted,
   And sealed the compact by *his* sacred grave."

   *   *   *   *   *   *

'Twas thus she spoke; but still in prostrate sorrow,
   While lowlier earthward drooped her brow august.
To-day is dark; vague darkness clouds to-morrow,—
   Ah! in God's hand the Nations are but—dust!

                    Paul Hamilton Hayne.

IN PACE REQUIESCAT.

    Hush, hush, speak softly,
The conflict now has reached the end;
   Life lies vanquished on the ground,
   Death with victor's wreath is crowned,
Oh, angels stoop—Oh, God defend!

    Toll, toll, toll, toll,
Ye brazen bells of woe and dread!
   Thy requiem send throughout all lands,
   Sweep on to distant ocean strands,
He lieth silent—lieth dead.

JAMES A. GARFIELD.

Gather, gather clouds,
Oh darkest clouds of sombre night ;
Lock the golden, smiling stars
Safe behind thy prison bars,
Grief wisheth not—nor beareth light.

Droop, droop, Freedom's flag—
Float not thy folds majestic, proud ;
Lie thou still across the breast
Of him the country loveth best—
It is a well-befitting shroud.

Yet, oh Columbia, free—
Up from the Past there rings the cry ;
"God reigns—the Government still lives !"
In the nation's heart, that honor gives,
He "only sleeps," he *cannot die*.

ONE THAT WILL BE MEMORABLE FOR GENERATIONS.

So back to earth, with fitting dirge, returns
More sacred mold than sleeps in royal urns !
A stricken nation bends with grief to lay
Upon her noble dead the amaranthine bay !
Of freedom's land a loved and laureled son !
The peer of Lincoln and of Washington.

His virtues
Will plead like angels, trumpet-tongued, against
The deep damnation of his taking-off;
And pity, like a naked new-born babe,
Striding the blast, or heaven's cherubim, hors'd
Upon the sightless couriers of the air,
Shall blow the horrid deed in every eye,
That tears shall drown the wind.

ELBERON.

Our brother craved a change, and by the sea,
    With calm, clear eyes he saw the ships go by,
Receding, coming, like the noiseless hours
    That trace the measureless eternity.
He slept to dream of morn, or waking, turned
    To see God's mighty work in light unroll;
The mist-stained stars still true, but faintly, burned,
    And sky and ocean met in one vast scroll.
If ever mind the sea's inscription read,
    That pure, deep mind with righteous Heaven communed.
The slender strip of shore, like life near sped,
    But all the rest with lofty hope attuned.
In love he sleeps, alone reprieved the pain,
That strangely surges round the world, again and yet
    again.

LAKE VIEW.

Once more the deep-stained line of blue meets blue.
    The restful waves in graceful motion curl ;
The clouds less rugged, and a tenderer hue
    Tinges the scene as day begins to furl
Its sunset banners. Here his eye has viewed
    The lordly lake whose whisper was of home.
Here he has known, in silent, solemn mood,
    The ashes of his love in time must come.
Full soon a shaft shall rise and many a crew,
    With blurring eyes, will watch it from the deck.
"His hands, like ours," they'll say, "hard labor knew,
    That column marks a glory, not a wreck.
He shows the power of virtue. Bless the land
That lifts the worthy toiler up, and trusts his sinewy
    hand."

THE QUESTIONING.

What is the lesson? Tears. Heart-molding tears,
    Known long ere history kept its blotted leaves.
The Gentlest One of all was pierced by spears
    Of human pride and hatred, 'twixt two thieves.
He taught the creed of love. That was too much.
    The age taught vengeance. It has passed away.
Go ask the veteran, struggling on his crutch,
    "Fought you for self?" "True men fight not that
        way."

What child is born without the agony
  Of motherhood? Atonement? 'Tis the law.
He whom we mourn no more on earth we see.
  Yet "much of Garfield's left." His name can draw
Nations together. Inter-knit, it dwells
A motive in the beating heart, whence human destiny
    wells.

J. W. M.

QUEEN VICTORIA'S GIFT.

From palace gate she looked across
  The sea, and saw a land in tears,
  And, calling back a few short years,
Was bowed with us and wept our loss.

True sister, mother, widow, queen,
  Thy love has touched a nation's heart;
  In sorrow thus to bear a part,
Thy grace and queenliness are seen.

Thy gift breathed o'er our martyr-dead
  Till ashes were with ashes laid,
  And two fraternal peoples paid
Their tribute with uncovered head.

All precious jewels fit and rare
  May sparkle in a diadem;
  Above all these there is a gem
That only royal souls may wear.

Dear oneness of all bosoms now,
    Since loss of Prince and President
    Has tears and prayers and spirits blent
As all in common sorrow bow.

What deep and wondrous ministry!
    Not eloquence of noblest lips
    Can speak the sacred fellowships
From love and loss and sympathy.

F. D.

PRESIDENT GARFIELD.

The hush of the sick room; the muffled tread;
    Fond, questioning eye; mute lip, and listening ear;
    Where wife and children watch, 'twixt hope and fear,
A father's, husband's, living-dying bed!—
The hush of a great nation, when its head
    Lies stricken! Lo, along the streets he's borne,
    Pale, thro' rank'd crowds, this gray September morn,
'Mid straining eyes, sad brows unbonneted,
And reverent speechlessness!—a "people's voice!"
    Nay, but a people's silence! thro' the soul
    Of the wide world its subtler echoes roll.
    O brother nation! England, for her part,
    Is with thee; God willing, she, whose heart
Throbb'd with thy pain, shall with thy joy rejoice.
    LONDON SPECTATOR, Sept. 6.   A. C. A.

REJOICE.

"BEAR ME OUT OF THE BATTLE, FOR LO! I AM SORELY WOUNDED."

From out my deep, wide-bosomed West
   Where unnamed heroes hew the way
For worlds to follow, with stern zest—
   Where gnarled old maples make array,
Deep-scarred from Red Men gone to rest—
   Where pipes the quail, where squirrels play
Through tossing trees, with nuts for toy,
   A boy steps forth, clear-eyed and tall,
A bashful boy, a soulful boy,
   Yet comely as the sons of Saul—
     A boy, all friendless, poor, unknown,
     Yet heir apparent to a throne.

Lo! Freedom's bleeding sacrifice!
   So like some tall oak tempest-blown
Beside the storied stream, he lies
   Now at the last, pale-browed and prone.
A nation kneels with streaming eyes—
   A nation supplicates the Throne—
A nation holds him by the hand—
   A nation sobs aloud at this.
The only dry eyes in the land
   Now at the last I think are his,
     Why, we should pray, God knoweth best,
     That this grand, patient soul should rest.

JAMES A. GARFIELD.

    The world is round. The wheel has run
       Full circle. Now, behold a grave
  Beneath the old, loved trees is done.
       The druid oaks lift up and wave
  A solemn welcome back. The brave
       Old maples murmur, every one,
"Receive him Earth!" In centre land,
       As in the centre of each heart—
As in the hollow of God's hand,
       The coffin sinks. And with it part
           All party hates! Now, not in vain
           He bore his peril and hard pain.

  Therefore, I say, rejoice! I say
       The lesson of his life was much—
  This boy that won, as in a day,
       The world's heart utterly ; a touch
  Of tenderness and tears : the page
       Of history grows rich from such ;
  His name the nation's heritage—
       But O! as some sweet angel's voice
  Spake this brave death that touched us all.
       Therefore, I say, rejoice! rejoice!!
           Run high the flags! Put by the pall!
           Lo! all is for the best for all!
                      Joaquin Miller.

REQUIEM.

Ohio gave her noblest son,
Her best, her bravest, purest one,
   To be the nation's head ;
She did not think, she could not guess,
That never more his feet would press
His native soil ; that he would come,
Shrouded, and motionless and dumb,
      And dead !

Thus once was yours, O Illinois,
The pride of giving, and the joy,
   The black, the bitter pain,
Of taking to your cradling heart
Dust, of your dust to form a part ;
The nation sent your murdered one,
As it has sent to us our son—
      Both slain !

He grappled with his direful fate,
And daunted death, that lay in wait
   For seizure on such prey,
Till death was won to be his friend,
And long forbore to bring the end ;
And as the day rolled slowly by,
We said, " O, God he will not die,
      But stay."

Raised to the honors of the earth,
He, with the treasures of his hearth,
   Went forth to be our guide,
To be our chief, we thought, for years,
And now, alas! we are in tears
Above a wan, unconscious face,
That we, in a sepulchral place,
      Must hide.

Ye black-draped banners, waving low,
The world is witness to our woe,
   And monarchs o'er the sea
Behold your wavering, star-sown blue,
Heavy with mourning's sable hue,
For him, who, could he speak, would say
Far wiser, sweeter words to-day
      Than we.

Since Lincoln died there has not been
So great a grief, so great a sin,
   So terrible a crime :
And yet " God reigns " is true as when
This kingliest of kingly men
Stilled a mob's frenzy, and the wrath
That would have left a storm-strewn path,
      One time.

" Come home !" dear son, Ohio's breast
Was ne'er so wounded, nor so blest,
   As it will be when thou

Shalt yield thy stainless clay to her
Who was thy truest worshiper ;
Within these borders thou shalt sleep,
While earth's brown coverlet shall sweep
    Thy brow.

Behind that wide brow's massive wall,
A soul, that man cannot recall,
    God had ordained to dwell.
Peace be to thee, thou weary one ;
Thy pain is past, thy work is done,
Beyond the sunset hills of life
Thou waitest mother, orphans, wife,
    Farewell!

'Tis a mighty lamentation sends its wailing through the air,
For a deeply stricken Nation is in mourning everywhere ;
And the South and North together bend beside an awful bier,
And, enclasping hands forever, seal their friendship with a tear.
We have thrust each other sorely on the battle-fields of yore,
We have turned the green earth ruddy with a crimson tide of gore ;
But the past is unconsidered in the shadow of the pall,

That, encurtaining our chieftain, has brought sadness to
   us all.
While the minute guns are firing, and the death car
   onward rolls,
We are marching, marching, marching to the camping
   ground of souls.
In the temple, whose high arches ring with heavenly
   greeting song,
We shall know why she "must suffer" who has borne
   this "cruel wrong;"
We shall know why our beloved in his hour of triumph
   fell,
And a world was left to wonder at this sorrowful
   Farewell.

Mrs. Laura G. W. White.

ILLINOIS TO HER BEREAVED SISTER.

Ohio, weep! let tears of blood
  Fall from your eyes like rain,
And we your sister States with you
  Will mourn your martyred slain.

Aye, weep, and don your sombrest garb,
  Habiliments of woe;
For never can your troubled heart
  A *keener* anguish know.

Oh, weep; nor sit with clasped hands
    And eyes so full of pain,
For tears will soothe the fevered brow,
    Will ease the tortured brain.

We, too, are mothers, and our hearts
    Have had, alas, to mourn
The loss of those most dearly lov'd,
    For they can ne'er return.

In vain we plead, in vain caress,
    Thou canst do naught but moan,
For from thy lips no words escape
    Save these, "No other one."

We look around in mute despair,
    We know not what to do;
Can no one break this spell, we ask,
    None cause the tears to flow?

A silence reigns, when from our midst
    Steps one with royal mien;
A golden crown upon her head
    Her robe a golden sheen.

With clasped hands and bated breath
    We pray success attend,
For if she fails we dare not think
    Of what may be the end.

One glance above, as from her eye
    A tear in silence steals,
Then with her queenly, regal grace,
    Advancing, stooping, kneels.

Ohio, sister, say not so,
    Say not "No other one
Hath grief like mine so deep to bear,"
    I, too, have lost a son.

A son, indeed, beloved by all,
    To me he was most dear;
But by the dark assassin's hand
    I am left mourning here.

I said at first, as now say you,
    This grief I cannot bear;
Turn whichsoever way I would
    It all was dark despair.

But now at last I have found peace,
    I neither sigh nor moan;
For I have found the strength to say,
    O Lord, Thy will be done.

The years have come and gone, 'tis true,
    Since he, my son, was slain;
So years will come again to you,
    And time will deaden pain.

I loved him then, I love him yet,
   And I will say to you,
Love *him* not less, nor him forget,
   For this you *can not* do.

But look around, and when you e'er
   Shall see another's woe,
Reach out a helping hand to her,
   And sympathy bestow.

And when in grief you're tempted sore
   To say, " No other one,"
O think of me and try to pray,
   "O Lord, Thy will be done."

The spell is broken; with the tears
   Fast falling down her cheeks,
Ohio clasps her sister's hand
   And tremulously speaks.

I will remember your brave son,
   And how he came to die;
And this will be to us a bond
   Of closer sympathy.

And children now unborn will tell,
   In song or eloquence,
Of those whom we so deeply mourn,
   Our martyred Presidents.

Illinois.

GARFIELD, PRESIDENT OF THE PEOPLE.

DIED SEPTEMBER 19, 1881.

What is this silence, that calls?
    What is this deafness, that hears?
The silence is Death. Like a voice it falls;
    It rings in the heedless ears

That never shall hearken again
    To the words of our blame or praise,
Nor the low-hushed moan of a Nation's pain
    As it rolls through the darkened days!

And the motionless body must yield
    To the spell of that hushed command.
Oh, that one of us, dying, had been the shield
    To save that life for our land!

Man that was trusted of men—
    Brave, and not fearing to die
More than to face life's meanness, when
    It clamored its partisan lie!—

Though you leave us, we lose you not!
    In the Republic you live
Sacred, and part of its deathless lot,
    For whose life your life you give.

Garfield—the name so plain,
    The name we know so well!
The name we shall never forget again,
    Of the man who for honesty fell!

Like another Winkelreid,
    You drew to yourself the spears
Of tyrannous hate, though yourself must bleed;
    And left us—our pride and our tears.

Legacy meet and rare,
    Of one who dared to be pure!
In the hearts of the people, who love what is fair,
    That precious renown shall endure.

O sorrow that falls like a stone
    In the midst of the calm of our peace,
As the waves of pity around you have grown,
    So may our truth increase!

                George Parsons Lathrop.
ENGLAND, September 20, 1881.

THE SOLDIER BY THE SEA.

Above the sea the stars were gently shining
    And twinkling in the night,
As life and death with brawny arms entwining
    Wrestled in weary fight.

Among the waves the winds were lightly sporting
    And laughing out aloud,
While death defeating life, and heaven thwarting,
    Had ready its white shroud.

The whispering waters hushed their idle prattle,
    The wild winds held their breath,
To watch the ebb and flow of the fierce battle
    Waged between life and death.

The earth and sky were silent in their sorrow—
    The end had come at last—
And burning tears of nature ere the morrow
    Told that the worst was past.

A soldier's soul had left its suffering pillow
    And gone out on the sea
Toward the stars so far beyond the billow
    Which beckon you and me.

Upon the sea the stars were softly shining
    And shimmering in the night,
As winds and waves their gentle arms entwining
    Wept sadly at the sight.
David Graham Adee.

GARFIELD.

He has fallen asleep. He is resting at last!
The pulse has grown still, and the fever is past.

He suffers no longer in heart or in brain,
And the pain that so racked him shall come not again!
    He has fallen asleep,
        And the fever is past :
    Thank god as you weep,
        He is resting at last!

O Mother, look now on the face of your boy,
The stay of your age, and your pride and your joy,
And plead through your sobs for one smile or one word
Of the lips locked in silence, unheeding—unheard!
    His dreams ere he died
        Were of home and of you,
    And he laughed and he cried
        As he dreamed of you, too!

And you, stricken woman, and wife of his heart!
What word did he speak ere he turned to depart?
Was it not the old love whose unwavering truth
In your old-growing hearts shone as bright as in youth?
    Yet so soundly he sleeps
        That he heeds not your moan,
    Nor the daughter who weeps
        With her brothers alone.

O country he loved, and who loved in return!
Let the flame in your mighty heart leap up and burn,

As you look on your son, who, in Liberty's name,
Must mix his pure blood with the blood of your shame—
    There he lies—unredressed!
    Without reason or cause
    Of his life dispossessed—
    Without justice or laws!

Did he fall in the right? Was he other than just?
Did he love not his neighbor as God said he must?
No! Even the dastard whose hand laid him low,
Though he pales as he answers, will answer you No.
    Stricken down! There he lies
    In the gray of the dawn!
    And with smiles in his eyes
    His assassin lives on!
Anonymous.

QUEEN VICTORIA'S WREATH,

PLACED ON THE LID OF PRESIDENT GARFIELD'S COFFIN.

In a land beyond the billows broad and deep and blue,
Sits the mighty queen of England, tender, great and true.
From across the sea and summer freighted winds have
    blown
Stories of the stars of diamonds, palace, prince and
    throne.

We have read in golden pages of the gracious queen ;
How the very sunlight glistens where her face is seen.
How the English roses richer spring beneath her feet,
As she treads the palace gardens or the vale's retreat.

Heraldry and deeds of valor down the Brunswick line,
Lose their splendor in the glory of the humble shrine,
Where she kneels to breathe a blessing, with her eyes
 of love
Lifted to the God of Heaven on that throne above.

But we never felt the tender touch of her fair hand,
Till the shadow of a sorrow fell across our land ;
Till it smote the mighty forehead of our nation's chief,
And the day of brightest glory darkened into grief.

Then it was her queenly bosom shared with us our pain,
And her messages of comfort were not all in vain.
But the token that shall never from our hearts be hid,
Was her simple wreath of flowers on the coffin lid.

They have faded ere these verses find a humble place,
But the sweet deed not the tempests even can efface
While the memory of our martyr president's great name
Holds a page upon the records in the halls of fame.

Geo. W. Ferrel.

JAMES A. GARFIELD.

AT THE PRESIDENT'S GRAVE.

September 26, 1881.

All summer long the people knelt
  And listened at the sick man's door :
Each pang which that pale sufferer felt
  Throbbed through the land, from shore to shore.

And as the awful hour drew nigh,
  What breathless watching, night and day!
What tears! what prayers! Great God on high—
  Have we forgotten how to pray!

O broken-hearted, widowed one,
  Forgive us if we press too near!
Dead is our husband, father, son—
  For we are all one family here.

And thou remember,—though relief
  Come not till thine own day grow dim,—
That never, in this world of grief,
  Has mortal man been mourned like him.

EPITAPH.

A man not perfect—but of heart
  So high, of such heroic rage,
That even his hopes became a part
  And parcel of earth's heritage.

Anonymous.

SEPTEMBER 19, 1881.

*In their dark House of Cloud
The three weird sisters toil till time be sped.*

I.

Clotho.—How long, O sister, how long
    Ere the weary task is done?
How long, O sister, how long
    Shall the fragile thread be spun?

Lachesis.—'Tis mercy that stays her hand,
    Else she had cut the thread;
She is a woman too,
    Like her who kneels by his bed!

Atropos.—Patience! the end is come:
    He shall no more endure:
See! with a single touch!—
    My hand is swift and sure!

II

First Angel—Listen! what was it fell
    An instant since on my ear—
A sound like the throb of a bell
    From yonder darkling sphere!

Second Angel.—The planet where mortals dwell!
    I hear it not . . . nay, I hear!—
A sound of sorrow and dole!

JAMES A. GARFIELD.

First Angel.—Listen! It is the knell
  Of a passing soul!—
  The midnight lamentation
  Of a stricken nation
   For its Chieftain's soul!
    Thomas Bailey Aldrich.

IN MEMORIAM.

Our best, our bravest, tenderest, dearest loved,
 Our knightliest son, untimely to the grave
By bitter stroke of cruelest fate removed,
 Not all our love nor all our prayers could save.
For weeks we fought the awful, stealthy foe,
 That menaced him with quivering poisoned dart—
For weary weeks, till hope beat faint and low,
 And gloom lay heavy on the nation's heart.

Our love for Garfield mated with our pride;
 He towered majestic far above the throng,
Like some tall pine that on a mountain side,
 By wrestle with the storms grows lithe and strong.
Heroic motherhood his cradle rocked;
 Heroic struggle nerved his ardent youth;
No siren false his stainless manhood mocked;
 To simple duty faithful, true as truth.

His was the leader's calm, undaunted soul,
    Too self-restrained to sway at passion's breath ;
His the grand fortitude that took control,
    And smiled a challenge in the face of death.
What matchless patience ! Tried with utmost pain,
    By anguish tortured, under weakness crushed,
Martyr and saint, he bore the fearful strain,
    Till in that presence lesser griefs were hushed.

Above his pulseless form what shadows bend !
    What glory wraps him, coffined, could we see !
The victors of the ages call him friend—
    Of Lincoln, Washington, the peer is he.
Columbia's hand shall write his name in light,
    Her sons shall lisp it by the hearth's red flame,
And generations hence shall measure height
    By this great man's white altitude of fame.

Still must we weep! We stand, the Thirty-eight,
    Joined hand in hand, with broken hearts to-day.
The mournful guns proclaim the mourning state—
    Its Chief, so foully, strangely reft away.
Droop lowlier, flags, to symbolize our woe !
    Toll slowlier, bells, and time you with our tears !
Tread softly, soldiers ! There are those shall go
    Uncomforted through all their lonely years.

Our leader fallen ! But his work remains
    Unfinished as he left it. East and West

And South and North arise the stern refrains
   That call his country to the hour of test.
No dwarfed ideal can we brook, who hear
   His voice serene and steady from the skies.
The listening air throbs palpitant, and clear
   Around us glows the fire of sacrifice.

IN MEMORIAM—JAMES A. GARFIELD.

Gone, our loved, our honored chieftain,
   Lowly droops the Nation's head,
While far o'er the whole world's bosom
   Weep the people for their dead.

Gone, with all the radiant future,
   Sweet as dream that poets sing;
Stately halls that flung their portals
   Wide to welcome in a king,

Now are shrouded deep in mourning;
   Flags at half-mast sadly rise—
But, ah! stricken hearts behold them
   Pointing ever toward the skies!

Garfield lives! the brave, the good,
   Hearts like his can never die,
Only gone from earth's green fields
   To the greener ones on high.

Bring the palm leaves and the roses
   From the sunny southern clime,
Place them with New England violets,
   And the laurel round them twine.

Fitting emblems for the soldier,
   For the scholar, and the son,
Nobly fighting in life's battles,
   Grandly was the victory won.

From his sleeping dust shall daisies
   Mingle with for-get-me-not,
And the odorous summer roses
   Glorify the honored spot.

And through all the countless ages
   God will grander records keep
Of the brave heart, hushed and silent ;
   Sweetly, then, oh ruler, sleep !

Abbie C. M'Keever.

J. A. G.

Our sorrow sends its shadow round the Earth.
So brave, so true ! A hero from his birth !
The plumes of Empire moult, in mourning draped
The lightning's message by our tears is shaped.

JAMES A. GARFIELD.

Life's vanities that blossom for an hour
Heap on his funeral car their fleeting flower.
Commerce forsakes her temples, blind and dim,
And pours her tardy gold, to homage him.

The notes of grief to age familiar grow
Before the sad privations all must know;
But the majestic cadence which we hear
To-day, is new in either hemisphere.

What crown is this, high hung and hard to reach,
Whose glory so outshines our laboring speech?
The crown of Honor, pure and unbetrayed;
He wins the spurs who bears the knightly aid.

While royal babes incipient empire hold,
And, for bare promise, grasp the scepter's gold,
This man such service to his age did bring
That they who knew him servant, hailed him king.

In poverty his infant couch was spread.
His tender hands soon wrought for daily bread:
But from the cradle's bound his willing feet
The errand of the moment went to meet.

When learning's page unfolded to his view,
The quick disciple straight a teacher grew;
And when the fight of freedom stirred the land,
Armed was his heart and resolute his hand.

Wise in the council, stalwart in the field!
Such rank supreme a workman's hut may yield.
His onward steps like measured marbles show,
Climbing the height where God's great flame doth glow.

Ah! Rose of joy, that hid'st a thorn so sharp!
Ah! Golden woof that meet'st a severed warp!
Ah! Solemn comfort that the stars rain down!
The Hero's garland his, the Martyr's crown!
Julia Ward Howe.

"HE IS DEAD, OUR PRESIDENT."

He is dead, our President; he rests in an honored grave,
He whom any one of us would gladly have died to save.
All is over at last, the long, brave struggle for life—
For a nation's sake, not his own, and for that of children
    and wife.
Doubt and suspense are dead, dead is the passionate thrill
Of a hope too blessed and sweet for aught but death
    to kill.
Do you remember yet, how, from that awful day
When the pulse of the nation stopped with a shock of
    wild dismay
And voiceless horror looked from questioning eyes to
    eyes,
As the murmur widened and spread "Our President
    murdered lies—"

How to the very last like a star in a night of gloom
The hope of the people burned till it sank in a hero's tomb?
We could not give him up—as a mother prays for her child,
We prayed for his precious life, with a love as deep and wild.
We had known him long and well as a man of royal mind
Who had nobly proved his birthright as a leader of mankind.
We had watched him, oh, so proudly! as in life's ranks he rose
By the fair and open warfare that endeared him to his foes,
But we never prized him rightly until he had meekly lain
Wrapped in speechless tortures of the fiery furnace of pain.
Then, how we learned to love him! for all that man holds dear,
For infinite faith and patience, and courage when death drew near,
For yearning love that strove with a pitiful, mighty strife,
To shield from the sting of sorrow the hearts of mother and wife.
Then with tearful vision, purged of passion and pride,
We saw in its tender beauty that spirit glorified,

And mighty love swept o'er us with a current as deep
    and grand
As the Nile that swells to a sea to nourish a hungry
    land.

O boundless sea of love and star of a hope that is dead,
Not vainly our President died, not vainly our loved one
    bled
If still that sea shall sweep onward which at first so
    narrow ran
Till the hands of the nation's clasp in the brotherhood
    of man,
Till the hate that smoulders still in hearts unreconciled
Shall change to the sweet affection that beams in the
    glance of a child,
And gladness shall dawn from sorrow, and glory burst
    from gloom
And the flower of love fraternal shall blossom from Gar-
    field's tomb.
Charles Turner Dazey.

THE SECOND MARTYR.

Hushed be thy moaning and sobbing, O sea!
    Thine but the semblance of sorrow!
And thou light-hearted as ever wilt be
    On the dawning for us of a bitter to-morrow!
O joyous sea! O bitter sorrow!

JAMES A. GARFIELD.

Ye winds appareled in midnight pall,
    How feebly ye voice his death
And harrow our hearts with the scenes ye recall,
    When he felt your bouyant breath!
O merry winds! O midnight pall!

O winds! and O sea! how sad to think
    That mortally-wounded man
Still cheerfully quaffed your breeze on the brink
    Where death's chill river ran,
And spoke in your praise, poor, patient man!

O Elberon bells! ye pierce the soul—
    He heard you with hope in his heart;
The hour for prayer he heard you toll,
    And ye caused his tears to start.
O hopeful heart! O Elberon bells!

Spirit of prayer! not in vain o'er the deep
    Of our sorrow thou brooded and breathed;
Lo! now we wonder, while yet we weep,
    At the blessings his battle bequeathed!
We weep and wonder, we wonder and weep.

No tears are shed for *him* in the skies,
    "Our loss," they know, "is his gain;"
Yet moist must have been even angels eyes
    To witness his wasting pain—
But no tears are shed for him *now* in the skies.

It is for the human heart to mourn,
    For human eyes to weep,
And aye for man of woman born
    To suffer and then to sleep—
It is for human eyes to weep.

O human hearts the world around!
    Stay not this torrent of tears!
For the love ye sow in his grave's holy ground
    Will blossom, for countless years,
In human hearts the world around.

By the desolate shore of this sea of sorrow,
    Trembling and mute they stand,
Who pray for the speed of a better morrow
    With their own in a happier land,
Where hope cannot die by the hand of sorrow.

A new-made grave, and a world bowed down,
    The while two martyrs meet
In the City of God! Behold the crown
    They have laid at a people's feet!
And men are moved when such martyrs meet.

Oh! his was indeed a martyr's doom!
    Thank God for the martyr's crown!
A cruel death and an early tomb,
    And unimagined renown!
God be praised for the martyr's crown!

                          D. M. Jones.

JAMES A. GARFIELD.

J. A. G.

HUMANITAS REGNANS.

With finger on lip and breath bated,
    With an eager and sad desire,
The world stood hushed, as it waited
    For the click of the fateful wire.

"*Better:*" and civilization
    Breathed freer and hoped again.
"*Worse:*" and through every nation
    Went throbbing a thrill of pain.

A cry at midnight! and listening—
    "*Dead!*" tolled out the bells of despair;
And millions of eyelids were glistening
    As sobbed the sad tones on the air.

But who is he toward whom all eyes are turning?
And who is he for whom all hearts are yearning?
What is the threat at which earth holds its breath
While one lone man a duel fights with death?

No thrones are hanging in suspense;
    No kingdoms totter to their fall.
Peace, with her gentle influence,
    Is hovering over all.

'Tis just one man at Elberon
  Who waiteth day by day,
Whose patience all our hearts have won
  As ebbs his life away.

His birthday waked no cannon-boom ;
  No purple round him hung ;
A back-woods cabin gave him room ;
  And storms his welcome sung.

He seized the sceptre of that king
  Who treads a free-hold sod ;
He wore upon his brow that ring
  That crowns a son of God.

By his own might he built a throne,
  With no unhuman arts,
And by his manhood reigned alone
  O'er fifty million hearts.

Thus is humanity's long dream,
  Its highest, holiest hope begun
To harden into fact, and gleam
  A city 'neath the sun :—

A city, not like that which came
  In old-time vision from the skies ;
But wrought by man through blood and flame,
  From solid earth to rise :—

JAMES A. GARFIELD.

Man's city; the ideal reign
   Where every human right hath place;
Where blood, nor birth, nor priest again
   Shall bind the weary race:—

In which no king but man shall be.
   'Twas this that thrilled with loving pain
The heart of all the earth, as he
   Died by the sobbing main.

For, mightiest ruler of the earth,
   He was the mightiest, not because
Of priestly touch, or blood, or birth,
   But by a people's laws.

O Garfield! brave and patient soul!
Long as the tireless tides shall roll
About the *Long Branch* beaches, where
Thy life went out upon the air,
So long thy land, from sea to sea,
Will hold thy manhood's legacy.

There *were* two parties; there were those,
In thine own party, called thy foes;
There *was* a North; there *was* a South,
Ere blazed th' assassin's pistol mouth.

But lo! thy bed became a throne;
   And as the hours went by, at length
The weakness of thine arm alone
   Grew mightier than thy strongest strength.

No petulent murmur; no vexed cry
Of baulked ambitions; but a high,
Grand patience! And thy whisper blent
In one heart all the continent,
To-day there are no factions left,
But *one America* bereft.

O Garfield! fortunate in death wast thou,
   Though at the opening of a grand career!
Thou wast a meteor flashing on the brow
   Of skies political, where oft appear,

And disappear so many stars of promise. Then,
   While all men watched thy high course, wondering
If thou wouldst upward sweep, or fall again,
   Thee from thine orbit mad hands thought to fling;

And lo! the meteor, with its fitful light,
   All on a sudden stood and was a star,—
A radiance fixed, to glorify the night
   There where the world's proud constellations are.

M. J. Savage.

WHY SHOULD WE MOURN?

Why should we mourn at death's alarms?
   His weary soul is gone to rest,
Reposing in his Saviour's arms
   And sheltered safely in His breast.
Away from pain and sorrow free,
Jesus, we yield him up to Thee.

LINCOLN AND GARFIELD.

A Nation mourns. Its flag is, sorrowing, furled.
   Nor faith, nor hope, nor love could save from death,
   Nor tears, nor prayers prolong the vital breath
   Of him, the foremost man of all the world.
Why should such shafts at such a mark be hurled?
   Inscrutable Thy ways, O Providence!
   And high above this place of groveling sense,
   Where mortals crawl and question God's intent!
And still "God rules"—and still "the government
   Lives on"—as when, in yonder Capital,
   Aforetime lay a murdered President!
Lincoln and Garfield! names forever blent
   The brightest blazoned on Columbia's scroll,
   Where "Washington" still glows with luster permanent.
                                          O. Everts.

GARFIELD.

So fit to die!   With courge calm,
   Armed to confront the threatening dart,
   Better than skill is such high art
And hopefuller than healing balm.

So fit to live!   With power cool,
   Equipped to fill his function great,
   To crush the knaves who shame the State,
Place-seeking pests of honest rule.

Equal to either fate he'll prove,
   May Heaven's high will incline the scale
   The way our prayers would fain avail
To weigh it—to long life and love!
London Punch.

THE NIGHT OF DEATH.

The tolling bells startling the silence of the night,
Proclaim the end.   Men gathered in the streets to hear
Yet more, when all is heard, and all a nation's might
Can do is now to weep upon his bier.

Some toil to shade in mourning's emblems dark
High pillars, mighty columns, that
The morn may greet a nation's grief;
And midnight comes and goes, and finds
And leaves them at their work.

                        But night
Had draped the continent in mourning ;
Save that the eternal stars shone forth,
And pierced the darkness of the vault.

Thus, in the shade of violent death,
Thus, from the darkness of the tomb,
The fame of him for whom our country grieves
Shall shine through all the gloom.
                    Rudolph Elstein Ugiets.

CARMEN AUGURATUM AUSPICANS.

(A PROPHETIC ODE AFTER SACRIFICE.)

O thou, my country, ope thine eyes
    Toward what the future holds for thee,
See the brave stripling rise
    From lowliest hut and poverty,
        From stair to stair ;
Nor hardly fix his footsteps there,
        Ere he another round
        Doth upward bound ;
Still, step by step, to higher stair
        Forward he leaps,
        Broader his vision sweeps,
Till he the loftiest summit gain—
    A people's hope to further and maintain.

But lo! as oft befalls the great,
  The wise and good,
There for a moment poised he stood,
Then passed beyond the gazing crowd
  Within the folded cloud.
    Wasted by weary pains
    His pale remains
    Now lie in state,
  Swathed in his bloody shroud ;
Peoples and kingdoms bathed in tears :
Hear'st thou the welcome greet his ears,
  As he his holier throne doth take ?
This Brave of fifty manly years,
  Dies he not now for thy dear sake ?

O follow then his leading far,
Be thou thyself the morning star,
Beaming thy glories round the world,
His name emblazoned on thy flag unfurled !
What speak the myriad bells,
Tolling this day their mournful knells ?
" Ne'er may our weight be swung,
Never our iron tongue
Slavery's base might extol
In town or capitol ;
But o'er a people brave and free,
Ring out in happier symphony,
    Garfield and Liberty !"
                    A. Bronson Alcott.

A HYMN.

Now all ye flowers make room,
Hither we come in gloom,
To make a mighty tomb,
   Sighing and weeping.
Grand was the life he led,
Wise was each word he said,
But with the noble dead,
   We leave him sleeping.

Soft may his body rest,
As on his mother's breast,
Whose love stands all confessed
   'Mid blinding tears,
But may his soul so white
Rise in triumphant flight,
And in God's land of light
   Spend endless years.

Prof. Swing.

TO MRS. GARFIELD.

Unsullied days with toil and struggle rife
  Will win at last; yea, God had given him all—
  A seat above the conflict, power to call
Peace like a zephyr o'er men's turbid strife;

Home music, too, children and heroine wife,
　　God gave—then gave Death's writing on the wall,
　　And on the road the assassin: bade him fall
Death-stricken at the shining crest of Life.

And yet our tears are sweet. God bade him taste
　　Honey and milk and manna raining down;
　　Clothed him with strength for good whose sweet
　　　　renown
Touched wind and wave to music as it passed;
Then crowned him thine indeed—giving at last
　　Heroic suffering, the true hero's crown.
　　　　　　　　　　　　Theodore Watts.

MIDNIGHT.

SEPTEMBER 19, 1881.

Once in a lifetime, we may see the veil
　　Tremble and lift, that hides symbolic things;
The Spirit's vision, when the senses fail,
　　Sweeps the weird meaning that the outlook brings.

Deep in the midst of turmoil, it may be—
　　A crowded street, a forum, or a field,—
The soul inverts the telescope, to see
　　To-day's event in future years revealed.

Back from the present, let us look at Rome :
　　Now, see what Cato meant, what Brutus said.
Hark! the Athenians welcome Cimon home!
　　——How clear they are, those glimpses of the dead.

But we, hard toilers, we who plan and weave
　　Through common days the web of common life,
What word, alas! shall teach us to receive
　　The mystic meaning of our peace and strife?

Whence comes our symbol? Surely, God must speak—
　　No less than He can make us heed or pause ;
Self-seekers we, too busy or too weak
　　To search beyond our daily lives and laws.

'Gainst things occult our earth-turned eyes rebel ;
　　No sound of Destiny can reach our ears ;
We have no time for dreaming——Hark! a knell—
　　A knell at midnight!　All the nation hears!

A second grievous throb! The dreamers wake—
　　The merchant's soul forgets his goods and ships ;
The humble workmen from their slumbers break ;
　　The women raise their eyes with quivering lips :

The miner rests upon his pick to hear ;
　　The printer's type stops midway from the case ;
The solemn sound has reached the roysterer's ear,
　　And brought the shame and sorrow to his face—

Again it booms! O, Mystic Veil, upraise!
　——Behold, 'tis lifted! On the darkness drawn,
A picture, lined with light! The people's gaze,
　From sea to sea, beholds it till the dawn:

A death-bed scene—a sinking sufferer lies,
　Their chosen ruler, crowned with love and pride;
Around, his counsellors, with streaming eyes;
　His wife heart-broken, kneeling by his side:

Death's shadow holds her; it will pass too soon:
　She weeps in silence—bitterest of tears;
He wanders softly—Nature's kindest boon,
　And as he whispers all the country hears:

For him the pain is past—the struggle ends:
　His cares and honors fade: his younger life
In peaceful Mentor comes, with dear old friends:
　His mother's arms take home his sweet young wife:

He stands among the students, tall and strong,
　And teaches truths republican and grand:
He moves—ah, pitiful!—— He sweeps along,
　O'er fields of carnage leading his command!

He speaks to crowded faces—round him surge
　Thousands and millions of excited men:
He hears them cheer—sees some great light emerge—
　Is borne as on a tempest; then——ah, then,

JAMES A. GARFIELD.

The fancies fade, the fever's work is past ;
  A moment's pang—then recollections thrill ;
He feels the faithful lips that kiss their last,
  His heart beats once in answer and is still !

The curtain falls : but hushed, as if afraid,
  The people wait, tear-stained, with heaving breast ;
'Twill rise again, they know, when he is laid
  With Freedom, in the Capitol, at rest.

Once more they see him, in his coffin, there,
  As Lincoln lay in blood-stained martyr sleep ;
The Stars and Stripes across his honored bier,
  While Freedom and Columbia o'er him weep.
                              John Boyle O'Reilly.

IN MEMORY OF GENERAL GARFIELD.

The long, brave fight is over ! To the last
  So gallant was the struggle made for life,
  We hoped a different ending to the strife ;
But death has triumphed ; and all hope has passed.

When night was darkest, 'neath the sobbing sea,
  From shore to shore the soundless message flew ;
  And in the dawn two kindred nations knew
That the brave general had ceased to be.

For weary months had he sustained the fight,
   Put face to face with Death he'd never quailed,
   Nor had his footsteps in the Valley failed,
For starlike had his faith illumed the night.

And now 'tis ended. Gone the gallant soul
   That to the last shone in his dauntless eyes;
   Left all unfinished is his great emprise,
And unattained his latest, noblest goal.

Yes, all too soon has he been stricken down,
   Too soon his voice been hushed, his strong arm stilled:
   Too soon, with wealth of promise unfulfilled,
Have immortelles replaced the laurel crown.

And yet the land had learned to love him well;
   And when a crazed assassin laid him low,
   'Twas a whole nation's heart that felt the blow,
A people round his bed stood sentinel.

'Twas a whole people waited day by day
   For tidings of the sufferer in his pain;
   And hoped and feared and feared and hoped again,
Nor ceased to watch, save when they 'gan to pray.

And 'tis a nation now weeps round his bier,
   Whilst from its kith and kindred o'er the sea
   There comes a burst of loving sympathy
For him the world mourns with grief sincere.

JAMES A. GARFIELD.

Columbia has worthy sons still left
   To fill the gap her murdered general leaves,
   But she remembers only him she grieves,
As o'er his corpse her vigil now is kept.

'Tis not her President alone she weeps ;
   No, 'tis an honest man, a soldier bold,
   A guileless statesman, never bought for gold,
That proudly she in sad remembrance keeps.

A loving father and a husband true ;
   A steadfast and an ever faithful friend—
   All these in him that she is mourning blend,
And all these fell when Guiteau fired and flew.

These lines, then, to the memory we pen
   Of him who's bravely met so dark a doom ;
   We lay them in all reverence on his tomb,
And join our tears with all his fellow-men !

                                Anonymous.

GARFIELD.

"DEATH LOVES A SHINING MARK, A SIGNAL BLOW."

O, let me seize the grandest, noblest strain!
Let me arouse my slow and sluggish brain !
O, let me grasp, with purest patriot grip,
The cup of inspiration, 'till my lip

Glows with unwonted fire, that my poor mind
May for a moment feel aroused, refined.
It is a solemn, sad, and sacred theme ;
So felt, so wept for, that I scarcely deem
That one so dull as I should dare to fling
His puny thoughts upon so wild a string!
But since I've touched the chord, I'll onward glide
With soul subdued, as one who mourns his bride.
The task is noble, or I fain would shrink
Into myself, feeling 'twere vain to think
Of shedding o'er that hallowed, lustrous name,
By such light means, a more enchanting fame.
He was the people's choice, and well they chose,
Prepared for distant and intestine foes ;
Proved in past times a brave and gallant chief ;
His honors mighty, but alas! how brief!
Short space for gladness, lo! how strange his doom!
A stricken nation mourning round his tomb!
Yet he shall live upon the burning page
Of distant time, a warrior and a sage!
Simple, serene, a man of wondrous skill
To win all hearts and mould them to his will ;
Austere in virtue, honest in each deed,
Sought by his country in her hour of need,
Snatched from the plow, the single-minded man.
She gave the highest gift a nation can.
High over all, majestic in his seat,
We shout aloud,—our hearts with triumph beat ;

And from the lakes, the mountain and the plain
Was echoed back the same exulting strain ;
And ev'ry bosom swelled with conscious pride
From fierce Atlantic's to Pacific's tide !

But mark the change ! Sounding from shore to shore,
Is heard the solemn bell and cannon's roar,
Is heard the question, quick response and sigh,
Wrung from our souls that one so good should die.
'Tis ever thus ; for fate with envious hand,
Plucks from the world the noblest of the land ;
Leaving false hearts and meaner minds to pour
Their venom forth, not having wings to soar,
And crawling onward, basking in the ray
Shed by their chief, yet dare to disobey
The people's voice, mocking its high behest
With viper spleen, tearing their mother's breast !

T. B. Coster.

FATHERLESS.

Over the land the tidings sped
"The leader has fallen, our Chief is dead,"
And over the land, a cry of pain,
Began, and ended with Garfield's name.

"He is dead," said each with tearful eye.
"So strong, so true, why must he die?"
   And the children paused that autumn day,
   To talk of the good man passed away.

Over the land, when the tidings came,
Even the babies lisped his name;
And youthful eyes grew sad that day
For the fatherless children far away.

Fatherless,—word with a life of pain;
Fatherless,—never complete again;
Always to miss, and never to know
The joy of his greeting,—his love below.

Missing the cheerful smile each day,
Missing his care in studies or play,
Missing each hour, each day, each year,
The sound of a voice so tender and dear.

Fatherless! only the children can tell,
The sound of that dreary funeral knell,
For only they, in all coming years,
Find the roses of youth bedewed with tears.

Over the land from shore to shore
The prayer of the children is echoed o'er,
"God of the fatherless, help we pray,
The wards of our mourning nation to-day."

Kate Tannatt Woods.

THE LAST BULLETIN.

Day after day as morning skies did flame—
  "How fares our Liege?" we cried with eager breath,
  "How fares our Liege, who fights the fight with death?"
And ever with fresh hope the answer came.

Until that solemn midnight when the clang
  Of woful bells tolled out their tale of dread,
  That he, the good and gifted one was dead,
And through his weeping land the message rang.

Then in the darkness every heart was bowed:
  While thinking on the direful ways of Fate,
  Where Love could thus be overthrown by Hate,—
"So wrong hath conquered right! we said aloud:

"If this be life, what matter how it flies;
  What strength or power or glory crowns a name;
  What noble meed of honesty or fame,
Since all these gifts were his—and there he lies

Blighted by malice! Woe's the day! and dead
  While yet the fields of his most golden clime
  Are rich in all the pomp of summer time,
With all their ripening wealth unharvested!"

*   *   *   *   *   *   *

Thus fares it with our Liege? Nay doubting soul,
  Not thus; but grandly raised to nobler height
  Of strength and power and most divine delight,
—At one swift breath made beautiful and whole!

Nor mocked by broken hope or shattered plan,
  By some pale ghost of duty left undone,
  By haunting moments wasted one by one,
But crowned with that which best becometh man.

Holding with brimming hands his heart's desire :
  While the fierce light of these last glorious days,
  Blazing on each white line of thought and ways,
Touches his record with immortal fire!
Marie E. Blake.

YOUNG GARFIELD AT CHATTANOOGA.

  I see bold Longstreet's darkening host
    Sweep through our lines of flame,
  And hear again, "The right is lost !"
    Swart Rosecrans exclaim.
"But not the left," young Garfield cries ;
    "From that we must not sever,
  While Thomas holds the field that lies
    On Chickamauga river!"

  Through tongues of flame, through meadows brown,
    Dry valley roads concealed,
  Ohio's hero dashes down
    Upon the rebel field.
  And swift, on reeling charger borne,
    He threads the wooden plain,
  By twice an hundred cannon mown,
    And reddened with the slain.

JAMES A. GARFIELD.

But past the swaths of carnage dire,
   The Union guns he hears,
And gains the left, begirt with fire,
   And thus the heroes cheer—
"While stands the left, yon flag o'erhead,
   Shall Chattanooga stand!"
"Let the Napoleons rain their lead!"
   Was Thomas's command.

Back swept the gray brigades of Bragg,
   The air with victory rung,
And Wurzel's "Rally round the flag!"
   'Mid Union cheers was sung.
The flag on Chattanooga's height
   In twilight's crimson waved,
And all the clustered stars of white
   Were to the Union saved.

O chief of staff, the nation's fate
   That red field crossed with thee,
The triumph of the camp and State,
   The hope of liberty!
O nation, free from sea to sea,
   With Union blessed forever,
Not vainly heroes fought for thee
   By Chickamauga river!

Hezekiah Butterworth.

AN EXILE'S TRIBUTE.

Dear native land in memory bowed,
Thy woe and grief upon us crowd!
Black burst the evil thunder-cloud!
And lifting—left us but a shroud!

And yet not so :—
The evil hand which struck the blow,
Unwittingly made strong the band
Of brotherhood, we did not know!
From every land—o'er every sea
Comes floating saddest melody
Of exiled ones who with thee mourn!
Of loyal hearts by anguish torn!

We mourn with thee our President,
But sadder still our eyes are bent
On one who stands alone!
We hear a widow's moan—
And longing, from this distant land,
We try to touch her gentle hand
      In human sympathy.

God lift her eyes to His great Day!
God lift her heart to Him alway!
God speak unto her heart in night—
And show His light.
              Mrs. John P. Morgan.

A BURIAL ODE.

We deck our hero for the tomb,
    And heap his bier with flowers,
While his grand spirit through the gloom
    Finds amaranthine bowers.

The favored State that gave him birth
    Receives her martyred son :
Carve deep the stone that speaks his worth,
    And tells the prize death won !

Let forge-flames die ! Let mill-wheels pause !
    Let traffic stay her hand !
Make bare your brow ! Twine sable gauze !
    Pray ye through all the Land.

Pray for his stricken family !
    Lament our nation's woe !
We have the whole world's sympathy—
    A true man lieth low.

We deck our Garfield for the grave,
    And hide his pall with flowers ;
His life, our love worked hard to save,
    Leaves " influence sweet " for ours.

                      T. G. La Moille.

OUR DEPARTED PRESIDENT.

Bear him back in silent sorrow,
    Place him 'neath his native sod;
There in angel's guard to slumber,
    Whilst his spirit rests in God.
Bear him back—the nation's hero—
    At her highest altar slain;
Hero on the field of battle,
    Hero on the bed of pain.

Bear him back, where his dear household
    To his tomb may oft repair;
Cherished mother, wife and children,
    Feeling that he still is near.
Bear him back, the struggle's over,
    Doubt and weariness and pain,
Though but few may be his cortege,
    Mourning millions make his train.

Bear him back, and though grief's passion
    Soon may be assuaged and calmed,
In the world's well-won affection
    Will his mem'ry be embalmed.
Bear him back, nor o'er his ashes
    Let a broken shaft be placed;
Life, though short, is nobly finished
    When with excellence so graced.

Bear him back, yet his example,
  Bright and true, and good and pure,
Ling'ring with the stricken nation,
  Through long ages will endure.
Bear him back, nor let faith falter,
  Though her prayers did not prevail ;
We must trust, in densest darkness,
  Him whose love can never fail.
                    Alfred Nevin, D. D.

LAY HIM TO SLEEP.

Lay him to sleep, whom we have learned to love,
  Lay him to sleep, whom we have learned to trust.
  No blossom of hope shall spring from out his dust,
No flower of faith shall bloom his sod above.

Although the sod by sorrowful hands be drest,
  Although the dust with tenderest tears be drenched,
  A feebler light succeeds the new light quenched,
And weaker hands the strong hands crossed in rest.

Our new, our untried leader—when he rose,
  Though still old hatreds fed upon old griefs,
  Death or disgrace had stilled the cry of chiefs
Of old who rallied us against our foes.

A soldier of the camp, we knew him thus ;
  No saintly champion, high above his kind,
  To follow with devotion mad and blind—
He fought and fared, essayed and erred with us.

And so, half-hearted, went we where led;
   And, following whither beckoned his bright blade,
   Learned his high will and purpose undismayed;
And brought him all our faith—and found him dead.

Is of the sacred pall, that once of yore
   Draped Lincoln dead, one mouldering fragment left?
   Spread it above him—Knight whose helm was cleft
Fair in the fight, as his who fell before.

As his who fell before, his seat we dress
   With pitiful shreds of black, that flow and fail
   Upon the bosom of the breeze, whose wail
Prays us respect the hallowed emptiness.

Ay! who less worthy now may take that chair,
   If our first martyr's spirit on one hand
   And this new ghost upon the other stand,
Saying: Betray thy country if thou dare!

Anonymous.

THE GREED FOR OFFICE.

Our every house is draped with mourning;
   Half-mast our sad flag flies;
Historic page for aye adorning,
   Entombed loved Garfield lies.

JAMES A. GARFIELD.

Loved more and more, as more we con him ;
    Each foul deed foiled with scorn ;
Greatness achieved, not thrust upon him ;
    High bearing, not high-born !

Small need to laud each noble feature ;
    World-wide his praises sound.
Death-stricken, now God's noblest creature,
    By greedy maniac's wound.

What haps to-day may hap to-morrow ;
    Our dead we can't restore.
Let's prove the semblance of our sorrow
    By doing so no more.

For, as we sit in dust and ashes,
    Rueing our mighty loss,
Perhaps this thought that o'er me flashes,
    Some other minds may cross.

This national office-seeking greed,
    At whose door lies the sin ?
'Twas madman wrought this special deed.
    Had *I* no share therein ?

Share in that vile plan we inherit,
    Which yields to clam'rous cries,
What to proved competence and merit
    Should justly be the prize.

                  Edward Berwick.

ENGLAND TO AMERICA.

Silence were best, if hand in hand,
   Like friends, sea-sundered peoples met;
But words must wing from land to land
   The utterance of the heart's regret,
Though harsh on ears that sorrow thralls
E'en sympathy's low accent falls.

Salt leagues that part us check no whit,
   What knows not bounds of time or space.
The homestead feeling that must knit
   World scattered kin in speech and race,
None like ourselves may well bemoan
Columbia's sorrow; 'tis our own.

A sorrow of the noble sort,
   Which love and pride make pure and fair;
A grief that is not misery's sport,
   A pain that bows not to despair;
Beginning not in courtly woe,
To end in pageantry and show.

The great Republic's foremost son
   Struck foully falls; but they who mourn
Brave life cut short, good work half done,
   Yet trust that from beyond death's bourne
That blameless memory's gifts may be
Peace, Concord, Civic Purity.

Scarce known of us till struck for death,
  He stirred us by his valiant fight
With mortal pain. With bated breath
  We waited tidings morn and night.
The hope that's nursed by strong desire,
Though shaken often, will not tire.

And now our sables type, in truth,
  A more than ceremonial pain.
We send Court, Cottage, Age and Youth,
  From open hearts, across the main,
Our sympathy—he never swerved—
To wife he loved, to land he served.

London Punch.

THE NATION WEEPS.

The nation weeps—the President is dead!
  And every heart is welling o'er with woe,
And droops in deep despondence every head,
  And every voice is tremulous and low,
  And even manly eyes with tears o'erflow,
For him who lies unconscious of the surge—
  A pulseless victim to the coward's blow—
While moaning waves upon the ocean's verge,
Join in the gen'ral grief, and sing the solemn dirge.

Alas, that he should die; so pure, so brave!
  So bright in all that dignifies a man!
So full of hope to help, to bless, to save;

And for his country's good to plan !
   His life's full pages all the world might scan,
And glean therefrom, in characters of light,
   His noble march from rear rank to the van,
Where he plucked honor from its topmost height,
And wore the laurel wreath full in the whole world's sight !

In vain, in vain, the universal prayer
   Ascended humbly to the heavenly throne,
Asking of God this single life to spare
   And save the nation from a cruel moan,
   And gladness spread to every peopled zone !
'Tis not for man Omnipotence to trace ;
   His motives to Himself alone are known ;
Meek souls with faith accept the offered grace
That moves his mercy throughout time, and tide, and space !

Though stricken hearts are bending o'er his form,
   And friends, and wife and children weep, with blinded eyes,
There will come comfort riding on the storm,
   To hush to rest their agonizing cries,
   And soothe to sadness e'en their deepest sighs !
He had lived long enough for fame to test
   His solid worth, his fitness for the skies—
God's justice numbered him among the blest ;
His mercy summoned him to his eternal rest !

                            Joseph A. Nunez.

THE SORROW OF THE NATIONS.

There's darkness over every land,
    The hearts of men are failing:
Man takes his fellow by the hand,
In nearer brotherhood they stand,
    For all the earth is wailing.

There's sorrow in the hut and hall;
    The bells of death are tolling:
The sun is hidden by a pall;
In whelming billows, over all
    The tide of grief is rolling.

Loved Britain's queen of grace and worth—
    The proudest thrones of power—
The millions high or low in birth—
Yea, all the peoples of the earth
    Are one in sorrow's hour.

'Tis not that bloody-handed war
    A nation's strength has broken;
No pestilence has swept the shore,
Nor famine left in any door
    Its grim and deathly token.

A cruel, vile, accursed blow
    The world's great soul has smitten;
It laid the man heroic low,
And lines of deep and bitter woe
    On countless hearts are written.

Up to the Majesty on high
    Unceasing prayer ascended
And kneeling millions wonder why
A righteous God should let him die
    For whom their prayers contended.

'Tis true a serpent strikes the heel,
    And man sinks down to perish;
And swift diseases from us steal
The loved and loving, till we feel
    This life has naught to cherish.

Yet, world of weeping! question not
    Whatever God ordainest:
He cannot err, no matter what
The seeming strangeness of the lot,—
    The Lord Jehovah reignest!
        Thomas MacKellar.

THE NATION'S GUIDE.

Half-mast the flag that long has waved on high
In joyous triumph to the smiling sky!
Another martyr claims the sign of woe,
Once more the Nation's heart is stricken low!
Once more throughout our mighty, mourning land,
From far off ocean strand to ocean strand,
The throbbing pulse of pain is wildly stirr'd,

And, trembling, shudders at the fatal word
That overflows with 'whelming weight of grief:
Garfield is dead—our country's honored chief!

His was a life sprung from the people's loins,
Whose humble boyhood with the lowliest joins;
Whose patient, strong endeavor, grasping mind,
Fixed purpose, and integrity combined,
By grand gradations sweeping on the tide
Raised him, at last, to be the Nation's guide;
Whose many virtues might our envy move
Were not each envious feeling lost in love.
May this his life from calumny defend:
He rarely found a foe—ne'er lost a friend!

Honored and blest have been his righteous days
Whose name descends on children's lips in praise,
By guiding, loving mothers fondly taught
To emulate his life in deed and thought;
Whose ever-living fame, from tongue to tongue,
Goes down the years in story told and sung.
O Patriot, Martyr, Husband, Father, Friend,
Thy work of life achieves this glorious end!

George Bird-Eye.

THERE IS MOURNING EVERYWHERE.

September, 26, 1881.

From where the Atlantic surges break on the rocks of
    Maine,

To where the prairie stretches its miles of golden grain,
From where the forests of the north sigh in their silent
  gloom,
To where the southern flowers in summer's beauty
  bloom.

The solemn bells are tolling for the nation's bitter woe,
And fifty million mourners are bowed beneath one
  blow ;
Through silent crowds and scattered flowers the funeral
  train moves past,
And after his long agony, our hero rests at last.

Call him not dead ; forever shall live that noble name.
High on the roll of honor, Columbia guards his fame.
With pride, and love, and pity, we give the " dust to
  dust."
In the hope of life eternal, with the God in whom we
  trust.

From beyond the restless ocean, come the words of
  England's Queen,
Who has known the same sad parting, the same bitter
  grief has seen,
And our kindred in the old home, clasping hands across
  the wave,
Tell us that we still are brothers, by our Garfield's open
  grave.

From the snows of mighty Russia, from Australia's far
    off land,
From France, our ancient ally, from the Roman pon-
    tiff's hand,
From Germany's great monarch, from the sunny fields
    of Spain,
From all come mournful greeting, all weep our hero
    slain.

But the wife's heart never falters, and her faith not
    once grows dim;
"He had reached earth's highest honor, and the Father
    called to him;"
He had fought the fight and conquered; he had won
    the golden crown,
And to wear that wreath immortal, he this earthly life
    laid down!

Anonymous.

OUR DEAD CHIEF MAGISTRATE.

Lake moans to lake, and sea to sea,
    Sad bells toll o'er the land,
The northern fir and southern pine
    As solemn sentries stand.

Our grand old mountains, hung with gloom,
    Bear up his pall to-day,
Our rivers chant his requiem
    Whose brow we crown with bay.

The Nations bare the head ; we bow
    Beneath the chastening rod ;
Our suffering ruler rests at last
    Upon the Mount of God.

Life's battle he had bravely fought,
    His shield with blood was wet ;
But tattered flag and "visage marred"
    Are more than coronet.

"Their works do follow them." We feel
    The heavenly promise sweet,
For his shall form a regal train
    To follow at his feet.

The truths he sought through mists of time,
    Full oft were veiled and dim,
But now he learns what they may know
    Who walk with seraphim.

And shall we wish him back to earth—
    Much as we longed to stay
His upward flight—now that he bathes
    In everlasting day ?

Back to the earth, whose day and night
    Are filled with deep unrest;
Nay, let us leave him where he lies—
    Upon the Saviour's breast.

Yet still with us his memory lives,
    Though he has passed on high;
"The nation's heart," O, soldier brave,
    "Will never let thee die."

S. A. J.

THE SOBBING OF THE BELLS.

The sobbing of the bells, the sudden death-news everywhere,
The slumberers rouse, the rapport of the people,
(Full well they know that message in the darkness,
Full well return the sad reverberations),
The passionate toll and clang—city to city joining, sounding, passing,
Those heart-beats of a Nation in the night.

Walt Whitman.

SONNET—JAMES A. GARFIELD.

Lo! as a pure white statute wrought with care
  By some strong hand, which moulds from Life and Death
  Beauty more beautiful than blood or breath,
And straightway veiled; and whilst all men repair

To see this wonder in the workshop, there!
   Behold it gleams unveiled to curious eye
   Far-seen, high-placed in Art's pale gallery,
Where all stand mute before a work so fair.
So he, our man of men, in vision stands,
   With pain and patience crowned imperial;
Death's veil has dropped; far from this house of woe
He hears one Love-chant out of many lands,
   Whilst from his mystic noon height he lets fall
His shadow o'er these hearts that bleed below.

                    H. Bernard Carpenter.

DUST TO DUST.

Two-score and ten! A broken life well spent,
The wise and good are glad such soul was sent—
By Him who giveth talents, one or ten,
To angels, mighty, and to mortal men!
Star of sun-lit age in lasting luster blent!
More radiant, now, in fairer firmament!

" Dust unto dust." From hallowed lips to-day,
These farewell words fall o'er the honored clay,
As back to earth, with fitting dirge, returns
More sacred mold than sleeps in royal urns!
A stricken nation bends with grief to lay
Upon her noble dead the amaranthine bay!

Of freedom's land a loved and laureled son!
The peer of Lincoln and of Washington.
Such names to struggling man bright beacons are,
As unto mariner the true pole star!
No cloud of time thy shining fame can mar,
But through all future gloom 'twill brighter glow afar!
James Nesbitt Karr.

AFTER ALL'S DONE.

His wife asked where was his pain. Garfield answered, "Darling, even to live is pain."

To live was pain—to die is peace;
   Falling asleep in tender arms:
     Ended vain hopes, more vain alarms,
Blind struggles for impossible ease.

Yes, life was loss, and death is gain;
   The martyr's blood the church's seed.
     O Christian, to Christ's world-large creed
Faithful till death!—die, rise, and reign!

Reign, king-like, o'er the souls of men;
   Shame them from paltry lust of gold,
     From public honor bought and sold,
From venal lie of tongue or pen.

Reign in the hearts of women brave,
   Fit mothers of the men to be;
     Like that true woman loved by thee,
Whom God so loved He could not save.

But thou art saved—her hero! Thine
   The glorious rest of battle won,
   A setting of the mid day sun,
And lo! the stars burst out and shine.

No long, dull twilight of weak age,
   Morn's glow forgot in misty night.
   Thy record was full writ in light,
And then—thine angel closed the page.

All's done, all's said. The tale is told.
   Across the ocean hands clasp hands:
   One voice of weeping from all lands
Binds the new world unto the old;

Then—Silence: and we go our ways,
   Work our small work for good or ill:
   But thou, through whom the Master's will
Was done, and didst it, to his praise,

Go straightway into eternal light!
   On earth among the immortal dead;
   In heaven—that mystery none hath read:
We walk by faith, and not by sight.

But this we know, or feel, half known:
   He who from evil brings forth good,
   His message, although writ in blood,
Has left upon thy funeral stone.

Miss Muloch.

THE DEAD PRESIDENT.

Braver than Roman sentinel
   He died enduring to the last ;
No captain ever nobler fell,
   Nor death a deeper shadow cast.

Prayers, none could reach the mystery,
   Though millions daily lifted theirs,
The morrow baffled yesterday,
   As if in scorn of tears and prayers.

He felt the deadly touch, and still
   With master-strength, he braved the strife ;
For, O, he battled with the will
   Of Christian fortitude, for life.

His courage won from all the world
   A hero's due, of homage great ;
At half-mast now, the flags unfurled,
   Are draped for him who lies in state.

Large brained, but larger yet of heart,
   His broadening sympathy divined
The lore of truth, and had the art
   To teach its lessons to mankind.

He sought no prize or praise of men,
   No selfish dream of blazoned fame,
His grand ideal of human ken,
   Was more than circumstance or name.

He saw beyond earth's narrow shore.
    And spurned the hollow sands of time;
For, in a higher faith he bore
    The spirit-life of trust sublime.

Alas, to honors, lifted high!
    Scarce one-half year of hope and fear—
In which to do, and then to die—
    Has laid him on his lonely bier.

A nation mourns beside the tomb
    Of him who kept its high decree,
Oh, death, thou hast thy sting and gloom!
    Oh, grave, thou hast thy victory!

S. H. Thayer.

BROTHERHOOD.

Drawn by the ties divine of sympathy,
The hearts of all the dwellers in our land
Have come together. North and South now stand
No more opposing, but in unity.
How strange a madman's murderous blow should be
The signal, bringing in on every hand
A flood of tenderness so pure and grand,
To prove the nation's heart-felt amity!
Ah, how unlike this generous brotherhood
Was that sad time when all the peaceful bands
That held our people in one common good

Were broken! Let the useful lesson be:
How sweet is peace and all its mild commands;
How dreadful war and all its misery!

Anonymous.

WHEELING, W. VA.

WHY SHOULD THEY KILL MY BABY?

The aged mother of the President is reported to have exclaimed as above upon hearing the news of his attempted assassination.

Why should they kill my boy—for he seems the same
    to me
As when, in the morning twilight, I tossed him on my
    knee,
And sowed for him hopes to blossom when he should
    become a man,
And dreamed for him such a future as only a mother
    can.

I looked ahead to the noon-time with proud but trem-
    bling joy;
I had a vision of splendor for my sweet, bright-eyed
    boy:
But little enough I fancied that when he had gained
    renown
Base envy's poisoned bullet would suddenly strike him
    down.

Why should they want to kill him? Because he had
    cut his way

Through poverty's gloomy woodland into the open day,
And sent a shout of good cheer to those who were yet within,
That honor is born of striving, and honesty yet can win?

Or was it because from boyhood he manfully bared his breast
To fight for the poor and lowly and aid the sore oppressed?
Ah! me, the world is working upon a treacherous plan
When he who struck for mankind is stricken down by man!

Or did they begrudge his mother the hand he reached her still,
No odds how high he clambered up fortune's glittering hill?
For in his proudest life-day he turned from the honors of earth,
And came and tenderly kissed me—the mother who gave him birth.

Shame on the wretch who struck him and grieves that it did not kill!
And pity for his mother, if she be living still.
May God in his mercy aid him his black crime to atone,
And help me to forgive him—I cannot do it alone!

Will Carleton.

AFTER THE JOURNEY.

AN INVOCATION.

O winds of heaven that sweep the land and sea,
  Now come with gracious healing on your wings,
And whisper to the sufferer tenderly
  Of rest, and health, and home, and pleasant things.

Blow strong, north wind, keen from the gulfs of ice,
  And balmy with the healthful scent of pine,
For thy pure breath holds medicine beyond price,
  And cordial richer than the rarest wine.

Or, west wind, if thou blow, then hither roam,
  O'er wide green plains and rustling fields of corn,
That thou may bring with thee a dream of home,
  And cattle lowing in the early morn.

But, south wind, come across the tossing sea,
  And blend thy perfume with its strong salt breeze,
So thy soft tones a lullaby shall be
  Unto the weary one, till sleep bring ease

And happy dreams to cheer his painful way,
  Sweet dreams of health and life begun anew,
So that, some hour awakening, he may say,
  At last! at last! Thank God, my dreams come true!

Anonymous.

THEY LOVED HIM.

Loud wails the wild September gale
   Across the land with solemn sound,
Adown the sky the dark clouds sail,
   The oak has fallen to the ground.

To day we stand with tearful eyes,
   For God has been more wise than we—
With folded hands our Chieftain lies
   Beside the sobbing Eastern sea.

By grateful millions loved and blessed,
   How glorious it is to fall—
To sink to death's eternal rest,
   So honored, so revered by all.

How grand to pass from his proud height,
   With all to speak his honest praise,
Into the fair and fadeless light
   Of brighter and of better days.

He sprang to life from lowly soil;
   He rose to honor and renown
By honest worth and manly toil—
   No weight could crush or keep him down.

We pay our tribute to his dust,
   We render homage to his soul;
His course was clear, his words were just—
   No faction held him in control.

JAMES A. GARFIELD.

How wise the way he firmly trod,
   How strong the purpose of his life ;
How true his trust and faith in God—
   His love of children, home and wife.

Through months of anguish and of pain,
   With failing strength and wandering mind,
None heard his pallid lips complain—
   He had no hatred for his kind.

And she whose presence made more bright
   His hallowed home, will always be
A ray of hope, a beacon-light
   To *all* on life's domestic sea.

With willing hands and helpful mind.
   She toiled and struggled by his side
Until the end. Still true and kind,
   She held his cold hand when he died.

Her name is honored everywhere—
   "The faithful friend, the worthy wife"—
A Nation will delight to bear
   The burdens of her widowed life.

Garfield, farewell ! your name is dear,
   The world is proud of your fair fame ;
No more the vile and envious sneer
   Shall fall when millions speak your name.

Your work is done, though incomplete,
　And undisturbed your dust shall dwell
On Erie's shore, where billows beat
　Along the land you loved so well.

And thousands yet shall seek that shore,
　As pilgrims seek some sacred shrine
Of holy saint whom they adore—
　Through endless years your life will shine.

In work you bore a noble part;
　Your feet were foremost in the race;
Your deeds shall dwell in every heart,
　Your manhood glorified your place.

　　　　　　　　Eugene J. Hall.

THE LORD REIGNETH!

The Lord reigneth, and the government at Washington still lives.—Garfield.

"Garfield is dead!" O thought so full of pain!
Hath death indeed then no regard for station?
Nor for the prince of virtues in the Nation?
Ah, he is dead! and yet the Lord doth reign.

Darkness and clouds are round about Him now:
We cannot understand, for they obstruct our vision,
But righteous judgment leads to each decision,
And *Love* lights up the frowning of His brow.

God is the stay of *each* and of the *Nation*,
Then blessed *he*, who in his reign believes
In death and life, in fear and tribulation.

There's naught, that in this hour comfort gives,
Save God, the *Lord* alone, and His salvation,
And but through Him our government still lives.
E. F. L. Gauss.

THE CALLING OF THE ROLL ON HIGH.

Sadly from the field of battle,
  To his rest a hero's borne,
Nobly hath he stood the conflict,
  Now to Christ his soul hath gone.
Bear him slowly, bear him gently,
  Lay the mangled body bye,
Let him sleep till Christ shall call him,
  Call and crown him, there on high.

Moan and break, O waves of ocean,
  Sigh, ye winds, across the sea,
While a mourning, weeping Nation,
  Gathers round the lifeless clay.
Marred and bruised, O piteous story,
  He so good, so soon to die.
But with Christ he'll stand in glory
  When they call the roll on high.

Faithful to the trust accepted,
    He by grace the crown hath won,
O, may grace to us be given,
    In his path to follow on.
Brave and true the Lord confessing,
    Self for him to crucify,
Ever ready to give answer
    When the roll is called on high.

Chorus.—Let him sleep, calmly sleep,
    While the days and the years go by,
Let him sleep, sweetly sleep,
    Till the call of the roll on high.

                      Anonymous.

SLEEP, COMRADE!

Illustrious dead! O glorious light,
    That wraps the soldier-statesman's dust!
    O broken scepter, keen but just,
That cleft the day out of the night.

Thou art no pillar fallen prone,
    No wreck upon Time's wreck-strewn shore,
    Thy name shall grow from more to more,
For all thy work was nobly done.

This was thy greatest; when you fell
   Before the greedy spoilsman's rage,
   You solved the problem of the age
And after history will tell

How the Republic rose and spoiled
   The spoilsman in his mad career,
   And wrought within this sacred year,
All that for which the nation toiled.

O noble offering on the shrine
   Of purer things and loftier days,
   Up from the darkness of the ways
Shall come effulgent light divine.

Here grief hath not one dark regret,
   Sorrow no bitterness of woe,
   And on thy turf the tears that flow,
Are gems in love's own beauty set.

Strong heart that quailed not at the cry
   Of harpies in their quest for blood,
   Brave lion, falling where you stood,
Thy great achievements cannot die.

O baptism red; O sacrifice
   Of greatness for the righteous cause,
   Truth, justice, better, purer laws—
Thy glorious monument shall rise.

In thy dead face we faintly see
   God's purpose of the after years,
   And, watered by the Nation's tears,
The harvest of the yet-to-be.

O comrade, tried on fields of fire,
   And true amid the battle's shock,
   Thy purpose firmer than a rock
Shall grow, the nation's one desire.

Till thy dead face shall rise and glow
   Like Arcturus in yon blue sky,
   A quenchless beacon shining high,
To point to us the path to go.

For her—God help her in her need—
   Who buckled on thy battle gear,
   And sent thee forth with smile and tear—
For her each soldier's heart will bleed.

For her—God help her while she weeps—
   Who crowned thee with life's proudest bays,
   When peace came with the shining days—
Each soldier's heart a vigil keeps.

Sleep on, O comrade of the sword,
   O civic hero, nobly crowned,
   Sleep till the last reveille sound,
While Fame and History stand guard.

Anonymous.

OUR FALLEN CHIEF.

We honored him, the good, while living,
    We mourn for him, the loved one dead ;
We join, in shrouded homage giving,
    The tears a stricken people shed.

Tears, whose source—a nation's sorrow—
    Our Chief in death's dark anguish lies ;
A gallant foe to-day—to-morrow—
    A friend in friendship's truest guise.

The great may die, the good forever
    Live on ; in nation's hearts they lie
Enshrined in love ; we may not sever
    His deeds from immortality.

Beside his bier no hates divide us,
    When one in grief all discords cease ;
His name the eternal star to guide us,—
    Beyond the gulf, to love and peace.

'Tis his—the diadem of glory—
    As when the great and good have died,—
To live in golden-lettered story,—
    Forever crowned, a people's pride.

                By an Ex-Confederate.

BURIAL OF GARFIELD.

A nation's head is bowed to-day,
    A world looks on in tears,
For one who pass'd from earth away
    In the glory of his years.
We lay his honored form in dust,
    Upon his native soil—
The great, the good, the wise, the just,
    A foul assassin's spoil.
So wondrous are the ways of God,
    So far past finding out,
We bow submissive to the rod,
    Without complaint or doubt.

Through years of gloom, from years of strife ;
    That found at last surcease,
Our nation had resumed its life
    Of union and of peace.
From North to South, from South to North,
    Waves of new feeling roll'd,
And the words on each that journey'd forth
    Were words we knew of old.
East turn'd to West, West turn'd to East,
    With looks of glad surprise,
As the bickerings of sections ceas'd,
    And we felt new hopes arise.

But now the orb whose steady light
    Fell everywhere—on all—
Has passed away from mortal sight,
    And shadows 'round us fall;
Yet we have strength, if we have will,
    Those shades to drive away—
The darkness to dispel, and still
    Enjoy the perfect day.
So let us, standing by the tomb
    That holds the honored dead,
Resolve to scatter far the gloom
    That threatens overhead.

Let us be MEN, not slaves to hate;
    Look warily about;
Prejudge not any one, but bate
    Our aptitude to doubt;
Look forward more than backward; see
    What *now* lies in our way;
Work for a day that *is to be*—
    Not for a vanish'd day;
Afar be all our bickerings hurl'd;
    Do as *he* would have done
Whom now we mourn, and show the world
    Though MANY we are ONE.

Anonymous.

AT REST.

A SONG.

At rest at last from life's sad toil,
   He's gathered in that fold
Where angels sing eternal praise,
   For valiant deeds and bold.
The clinging arms that held him dear,
   Have loosed their loving hold;
The heart that throbb'd in gratitude,
   Is silent now and cold.

But while we weep and vainly mourn,
   Our loss, our country's pride,
The heavenly choir with golden harps
   Sing welcome at his side,—
A good and faithful servant to
   "His Lord has entered in."
They bid us dry our tears for him
   Who came, his crown to win.

Arise then, see the Master's hand
   E'en in this bitter blow;
Be sure the perfect time has come,—
   All else, ye cannot know.
Firm at the helm he stood his own,
   Steadfast, and firm, and true;
Unswerving in his manly course,
   No matter what wind blew.

JAMES A. GARFIELD.

A Nation's hope was granted him,
    A Nation's trust and care ;
A martyr at his post he fell,
    Lost in a cruel snare.
And now a mighty Nation mourns
    All that was brave and best ;
His earnest, Christian deeds will live
    To sanctify his rest.
B. Herbert.

A LITTLE WHILE.

A little while shall loved ones dwell apart ;
Only a little while, and then
The messenger will come again,
And coming, call for thee, my friend,
And thou wilt follow willingly.

Waiting this little while in some still hour,
The spirit freed from clay will have
Permit to come and sit with thee ;
With unseen hand to lead thee on,
And cheer thee in thy loneliness.

Wait patiently the while, the one now gone,
Will be, perchance, close by thy side
When thou shall pass the stream of death ;
Will be the first to take thy hand,
When thou shalt enter Paradise.

This little while all past, no parting more
For thou and thine; the faith was had
In Him, Immanuel will bring
Each to a heavenly Father's home,
Where dwells our Lord, our Righteousness.
P. H. Taylor.

TIME'S HAND SHALL COMFORT US.

Consigned to earth. The last sad rite is o'er;
   The solemn bells at length have ceased to toll.
The stricken nation sits with bended head,
   For, still reverberating through its soul,
Are mournful echoes of the bell's sad chime,
And only can the healing hand of Time
      Reach down to comfort us.

That great, calm soul has found the Infinite.
   The brave, true heart, that only sought His will
And the nation's good, shall throb no more;
   Its work is done. The finite hand is still.
But is he dead? he whom the nation weeps?
"Be still, and watch, ye sufferers, he but sleeps."
      Time's hand shall comfort us.

For he has left, as priceless legacy,
   A spotless fame, a tender love and pure,
A deep devotion to a noble cause,
   Undying faith that right shall still endure.

And after patience, hope and courage lie,
Bereft of strength, and only wait to die,
    Knows time shall comfort us.

Oh, from those heights beyond our ken,
    To which thine eagle soul hath flown,
Canst thou look back to haunts of men,
    And know us as we would be known?
Then shall thou see how deep our love
    For thee, and all thy heart loved best,
Our earnest lives would gladly prove
    The nation honors thy bequest.

From the dim future comes a potent voice:
    "The nation shall not cry to God in vain;
He did not die who seemed to sleep,
    I called him, but he came that he might reign
In grander state; the little pomp below
    Was not for such as he. 'Tis empty show.
        Time's hand shall comfort thee."

Lucy M. Creemer.

THOU KNOWEST BEST.

Thy will be done! We cannot lift the veil
That shrouds thy wisdom, Lord, from mortal eyes.
Thou art unfathomable, and Thy ways
Past finding out.

In grief we humbly bow
As tear-dimmed eyes behold our stricken Chief
Laid low by death.   In vain we try to grasp
The lesson Thou wouldst teach a sorrowing world :
The arm that oft has stayed the approaching tide
Of party feud and strife no longer holds
The helm ; the mind, replete with golden thought,
Forever striving after clearer truth
And light, is now at rest ; the tender heart,
Aglow with love, and aspirations grand,
Is cold and still.   Around their leader's bier
A mourning nation weeps; whilst faith and doubt
And love and fear presume, with contrast strange,
To solve the mystery of Thy providence.
But Thou knowest best, and once, when face to face
We see no longer darkly through the glass,
We, too, shall know.   Death's call brooks no delay,
It comes to all.   And as the parents' hearts
Are joined more firmly o'er a loved one's grave,
So o'er our chief to-day, now cold in death,
A nation's union is more strongly knit.
From East and West, from North and South, the hearts
Of millions beat as one with poignant grief,
And faction's angry voice is hushed once more.
   * * * * * * *
We leave in faith and hope our doubts, our fears,
Our country's future destiny, our all
With Thee, our Father, and our country's God.
F. W. Reeder.

"STRANGE CRAFT IN THE OFFING."

Impatient while we weep they wait,
Three shining angels, white and great,—
Three galleys riding brave in bay
To bear our ruler's soul away.

All men might see the first that came,
A messenger of lucent flame,
And watch how strangely, day by day,
The great ship neared or wore away.

And, lo! a fourth, as sudden sent,
On errand grand and imminent,
Were not our ears too dull to hear
We well might note her hailing cheer!

Oh, wondrous ships, whose airy spars
Unseen float by the sentry stars,
And but for those great lights and fair
Would come upon us unaware!

Save that from waves auroral rolled
The air is full of dirges tolled ;
Save that from cottage and from tower
One sable woe is signed this hour,

E'en while we wonder and look on
To fairer isles than Avalon,
Ye bear the ruler of this land
And furl your sails on heaven's strand.

Lillie C. Darst.

GARFIELD'S FAVORITE HYMN.

Ho, reapers of life's harvest,
   Why stand with rusted blade,
Until night draws around thee,
   And day begins to fade?
Why stand ye idle, waiting
   For reapers more to come?
The golden morn is passing,
   Why sit ye idle, dumb?

Thrust in your sharpened sickle,
   And gather in the grain;
The night is fast approaching,
   And soon will come again.
Thy master calls for reapers;
   And shall he call in vain?
Shall sheaves lie there ungathered,
   And waste upon the plain?

Come down from hill and mountain,
   In morning's ruddy glow,
Nor wait until the dial
   Points to the noon below:
And come with the strong sinew,
   Nor faint in heat or cold;
And pause not till the evening
   Draws round its wealth of gold.

A LETTER FROM JOHN G. WHITTIER.

In reply to an invitation to contribute a memorial poem, Mr. Whittier responded in the following brief letter which is poetical in its sympathy, and expresses with pathos, the sadness of his great heart in this our nation's calamity:

Danvers, Mass., 10*th mo.*, 19, 1881.

J. C. McCLENAHAN,

Dear Friend:—Owing to illness, I have been under the necessity of abstaining from literary work for some time, and, while I have deeply felt the occasion, I have not been able to write memorial verse on the death of our beloved President. I enclose a letter of mine on the subject, which will show that I share the sorrow and sympathy felt so deeply and widely.

Thy Friend,

JOHN G. WHITTIER.

Danvers, Mass., 9*th mo.*, 24, 1881.

W. H. B. CURRIER,

My Dear Friend:—I regret that it is not in my power to join the citizens of Amesbury and Salisbury in the memorial services on the occasion of the death of our lamented President. But, in heart and sympathy, I am with you. I share the great sorrow which overshadows the land; I fully appreciate the irretrievable loss. But it seems to me, that the occasion is one for thankfulness as well as grief. Through all the stages of the solemn tragedy which has just closed with the death of our noblest and best, I have felt that the Divine

Providence was over-ruling the mighty affliction—that the patient sufferer at Washington was drawing with cords of sympathy all sections and parties nearer to each other. And now when South and North, Democrat and Republican, Radical and Conservative, lift their voices in one unbroken accord of lamentation; when I see how, in spite of the greed of gain, the lust of office, the strifes and meanness of party politics, the great heart of the nation proves sound and loyal, I feel a new hope for the republic, I have a firmer faith in its stability. It is said that no man liveth and no man dieth to himself; and the pure and noble life of Garfield, and his slow, long martyrdom, so bravely borne in the view of all, are, I believe, bearing for us as a people, "the peaceful fruits of righteousness." We are stronger, wiser, better for them.

With him it is well. His mission fulfilled, he goes to his grave by the Lakeside, honored and lamented as man never was before. The whole world mourns him. There is no speech nor language where the voice of his praise is not heard. About his grave gather, with heads uncovered, the vast brotherhood of man.

And with us it is well, also. We are nearer a united people than ever before. We are at peace with all; our future is full of promise; our industrial and financial condition is hopeful. God grant that, while our material interests prosper, the moral and spiritual influence of this occasion may be permanently felt; that the solemn sacrament of sorrow whereof we have been made partakers, may be blest to the promotion of the "righteousness which exalteth a nation."

Thy Friend,
JOHN G. WHITTIER.

POEMS BY JAMES A. GARFIELD.

The following poems, written by MR. GARFIELD, show something of his poetic inspiration, as well as his broad native gifts and consummate culture. The poem "Memory" was written before our late President's first term in Congress,—hence some twenty years ago, and is worthy of the great fame of its author. At that time possibly the president of a Christian college was the "summit where the sunbeams fell," but the last lines are all but a prophecy. The other, entitled "Autumn," written while a student at Williams College, is singularly touching, embracing with comprehensive sympathy his love for the beautiful and harmonious in nature.

MEMORY.

'Tis beauteous night! the stars look brightly down
Upon the earth, decked in her robe of snow.
No light gleams at the window, save my own,
Which gives its cheer to midnight and to me.
And now, with noiseless step, sweet memory comes
And leads me gently through her twilight realms.
What poet's tuneful lyre has ever sung
Or delicate pen e'er portrayed,
The enchanted, shadowy land where memory dwells?
It has its valleys, cheerless, lone and drear,
Dark-shaded by the mournful cypress tree;

And yet its sun-lit mountain-tops are bathed
In Heaven's own blue.   Upon its craggy cliffs,
Robed in the distant light of dreamy years,
Are clustered joys serene of other days.
Upon its gentle, sloping hillsides bend
The weeping willows o'er the sacred dust
Of dear departed ones! yet in that land,
Where'er our footsteps fall upon the shore,
They that were sleeping rise from out the dust
Of death's long, silent years, and round us stand
As erst they did before the prison tomb
Received their clay within its voiceless halls.
The heavens that bend above that land are hung
With clouds of various hues.   Some dark and chill,
Surcharged with sorrow, cast with somber shade
Upon the sunny, joyous land below.
Others are floating through the dreamy air,
White as the falling snow, their margins tinged
With gold and crimsoned hues; their shadows fall
Upon the flowery meads and sunny slopes,
Soft as the shadow of an angel's wing.
When the rough battle of the day is done,
And evening's peace falls gently on the heart,
I bound away across the noisy years,
Unto the utmost verge of memory's land,
Where earth and sky in dreamy distance meet,
And memory dim with dark oblivion joins,
Where woke the first remembered sounds that fell

Upon the ear in childhood's early morn;
And, wandering thence along the rolling years,
I see the shadow of my former self
Gliding from childhood up to man's estate.
The path of youth winds down through many a vale,
And on the brink of many a dread abyss,
From out whose darkness comes no ray of light,
Save that a phantom dances o'er the gulf
And beckons toward the verge. Again the path
Leads o'er the summit where the sunbeams fall;
And thus in light and shade, sunshine and gloom,
Sorrow and joy, the life-path leads along.

AUTUMN.

Old Autumn thou art here! Upon the earth
And in the heavens the signs of death are hung;
For o'er the earth's brown breast stalks pale decay,
And 'mong the lowering clouds the wild winds wail,
And sighing sadly, shout the solemn dirge
O'er summer's fairest flowers, all faded now.
The winter god, descending from the skies,
Has reached the mountain tops and decked their brows
With glittering frosty crowns, and breathed his breath
Among the trumpet-pines, that herald forth
His coming.

Before the driving blast
The mountain oak bows down his hoary head,
And flings his withered locks to the rough gales
That fiercely roar among his branches bare,
Uplifted to the dark, unpitying heavens.
The skies have put their mourning garments on,
And hung their funeral drapery on the clouds.
Dead nature soon will wear her shrouds of snow,
And lie entombed in winter's icy grave.

Thus passes life. As heavy age comes on,
The joys of youth—bright beauties of the spring—
Grow dim and faded, and the long dark night
Of death's chill winter comes. But as the spring
Rebuilds the ruined wrecks of winter's waste,
And cheers the gloomy earth with joyous light
So o'er the tomb the star of hope shall rise
And usher in an ever-during day.

www.ingramcontent.com/pod-product-compliance
Lightning Source LLC
Chambersburg PA
CBHW030356170426
43202CB00010B/1396